WHAT PEOPLE ARE SAYING
ABOUT *THRILL SEQUENCE* . . .

"Coming from a pastor with a wide range of experiences in leadership and faith, Rob brings a fresh perspective to the table. In his newest book, *Thrill Sequence,* he demonstrates how to make the faith experience something of authentic and lasting significance, rather than a fleeting series of thrills."

JOHN C. MAXWELL

#1 New York Times *bestselling author and leadership expert; founder of the John Maxwell Company*

"As Jane said to Tarzan as he left for work, 'Don't forget to hang on to the vine.' If you want to experience the thrill of the jungle—and not just toothless tigers tamed for the circus or caged and staged simulations—Rob Ketterling can show you how to hang on to the Vine."

LEONARD SWEET

bestselling author of over sixty books, professor (Drew University, George Fox University, Tabor College), and chief contributor to sermons.com

"Rob Ketterling is one of my favorite people on the planet. I love his writing too! If you're looking to take your faith to the next level, Rob's latest work is a "can't miss.""

MARK BATTERSON

New York Times *bestselling author of* The Circle Maker

"*Thrill Sequence* is a true joy to read! Delivered with passion, truth, and love, this book is sure to strengthen your faith and trust in God. Pastor Rob shares hope and encouragement that will bring new excitement and energy to your life—so you can run your race the way it was always meant to be!"

CHRISTINE CAINE
Founder of The A21 Campaign, bestselling author of Unstoppable

"If you're looking to take your faith to the next level, Rob's latest work is a 'can't miss.' This is a truly unique and helpful resource for small groups, Bible studies, congregations, and leadership teams alike. Let's learn to be reckless with our lives and live the adventure God always intended for us!"

WILFREDO "CHOCO" DE JESÚS
Senior Pastor, New Life Covenant Church, Chicago, Illinois;
author of In the Gap *and* Amazing Faith

"Rob's new book, *Thrill Sequence,* sets you free to live fully for God. He teaches you how to have a life of lasting joy, freedom, and excitement. *Thrill Sequence* is filled with encouragement, passion, and understandable application for life. Rob shares personal stories and writes with power and inspiration in a life-changing way!"

NANCY ALCORN
Founder and President of Mercy Ministries

"Serving Jesus is adventuresome and takes a reckless faith. Just ask the apostles—they performed death defying acts of courage to take the gospel to the ends of the earth, and it gave them a thrill that lasts for eternity. In his new book, *Thrill Sequence,* Rob Ketterling shows the difference between human thrill seeking and the rush of adrenaline that comes with it, and a radically different kind of thrill like what the apostles experienced as they lived in the higher realm of the Spirit—much different and far better than the pointless pursuit of human thrills. Following Jesus is truly thrilling. Thanks again Rob for helping us see the higher realm!"

GORDON ANDERSON, PHD

President, North Central University, Minneapolis, Minnesota

"As a young youth leader in my ministry many years ago, Rob Ketterling possessed a supernatural mark of greatness and God-placed potential. His life, his faith and his passion is contagiously wrapped in this book. Time to take a 'thrill' ride into the unknown!"

GLEN BERTEAU

Senior Pastor, The House Modesto, Modesto, California

"For those that want to finish strong and not just start strong, this is the book for you. My friend Rob Ketterling shares in his book *Thrill Sequence* how to live by faith and not just temporary thrills. These aren't just great principles for life; I have seen Rob live them out. Every pastor and leader should get this book and share with your team."

MATT FRY

Lead Pastor, C3 Church, Clayton, North Carolina

"The call to follow Jesus was never meant to be boring or mundane. It's a life of raw faith and real adventure. Rob Ketterling challenges us to discover the true thrill in following Jesus in his newest book, *Thrill Sequence*. Read this book today and you won't be the same!"

STOVALL WEEMS

Lead Pastor, Celebration Church, Jacksonville, Florida

"Rob Ketterling's new book *Thrill Sequence* will jolt you out of the spiritual doldrums with a long-lasting burst of fresh insight on your relationship with God. With strong biblical wisdom, leadership take-aways, and inspiring examples, Rob's book will catapult your faith to the next level. Individuals, small groups, and entire church communities will love reading *Thrill Sequence*."

CHRIS HODGES

Senior Pastor, Church of the Highlands, Birmingham, Alabama; author of Fresh Air *and* Four Cups

"Coming from a pastor with a wide range of experiences in leadership and faith, Rob brings a fresh perspective to the table. In his newest book, *Thrill Sequence,* he demonstrates how to make the faith experience something of authentic and lasting significance, rather than a fleeting series of thrills."

ROD LOY

Senior Pastor, First Assembly of God North Little Rock, Arkansas; author of Three Questions *and* Immediate Obedience

"I have known Rob for over fifteen years and as an incredible pastor, leader, husband, and father he brings a fresh, much needed, perspective to the table. In his newest book, *Thrill Sequence,* he demonstrates how to make the faith experience the way Christ intended it to be: authentic with lasting significance, rather than a shallow and fleeting series of thrills."

LEE DOMINGUE

CEO, Kingdom Builders U.S., Founder, Trafficking Hope & Hope House U.S. author; Pearls of the King

"As with his previous bestseller, *Change Before You Have To,* Rob captures, in his new book, *Thrill Sequence,* an essence that will truly captivate you and compel you to greater feats in Christ. The rawness and authenticity on each page are only matched by the books clarity and helpfulness in catalyzing change in the heart of the reader. You'll be glad you picked this one up!"

MICHAEL MURPHY
Founding Director, Leaderscape

"Children will jump off a wall into the outstretched arms of their parents and repeat it as often as the parents can handle it. They love thrill sequences. Why does getting older, or rather more mature, mean we start to play it safe? When do we start playing not to lose rather than playing to win? My friend Rob Ketterling, in his book *Thrill Sequence,* will help you understand what it means to live an abandoned life of faith and experience more thrill sequences than you ever imagined. Reading this book will challenge you to go after the incredible adventure serving God was always meant to be!"

DR. SAM CHAND
Leadership Consultant and author of Leadership Pain;
www.samchand.com

"Rob Ketterling is first and foremost a pioneer in the arena of faith. In a world that is over-managed and under-led, Rob is somewhere way out in front of the pack motioning for the rest of us to 'come this way.' As you read the pages of this book you will first hear him and then see him in the distance. Put your seatbelt on, you're in for the ride of your life."

RICH WILKERSON
Senior Minister, Trinity Church, Miami, Florida

"My friend Rob Ketterling is a leader and man of God whose experiences have given him a fresh perspective on what it means to follow Jesus. So many people are wearing themselves out seeking one temporary thrill after another. Through this book, Rob will help you embark on a faith adventure that lasts."

JOHN BEVERE

bestselling author; minister, Messenger International

"What do you chase after? What do you need to give you a rush? No matter where we get our thrills, they never last for long. That's because, as Rob reminds us, they are only hints of what God really wants for our lives. Check out *Thrill Sequence* and learn what it means to chase after a God who offers us more than we could ever imagine."

GREG SURRATT

founding pastor, Seacoast Church, Charleston, South Carolina

"Even if you don't realize that you're tired of going through the motions of ministry, this book will reignite your faith and awaken a passionate recklessness that we all long for deep inside our spirits. Be ready for a new adventure with Rob's latest authentic thought-provoking resource."

RANDY BEZET

Lead Pastor, Bayside Community Church, Bradenton, Florida

"Coming from a pastor with a wide range of experiences in leadership and faith, Rob brings a fresh perspective to the table. In his newest book, *Thrill Sequence,* he demonstrates how to make the faith experience something of authentic and lasting significance, rather than a fleeting series of thrills."

SCOTT WILSON

*Senior Pastor, The Oaks Fellowship, Red Oak, Texas;
author* Ready, Set, Grow

"The adventure laid out in my friend Rob Ketterling's newest book, *Thrill Sequence,* is about finding the ultimate thrill of a reckless faith. The message is backed up with solid biblical truth of how God wants us to consistently grow higher and deeper in a joyful faith, rather than live life searching for the next momentary high. Rob's message inspires and encourages a resolute belief in Christ and explains what it means to have bold and everlasting faith in a world full of short, cheap thrills."

ROBERT MORRIS

founding Senior Pastor, Gateway Church; bestselling author of
The Blessed Life, From Dream to Destiny, *and* The God I Never Knew

"It can be easy to get comfortable and play it safe in so many areas of our lives. *Thrill Sequence* carries an engaging and compelling message about the power of reckless faith. Rob's words inspire us to cast our fears, reservations and rationalizations aside and throw ourselves fully into an all-in faith journey with God."

JOHN SIEBELING

Lead Pastor, The Life Church, Memphis, Tennessee

"In *Thrill Sequence*, my friend Rob Ketterling takes a unique angle on living the life you've always said you wanted to live. This book will help readers everywhere break the cycle of sameness and truly live the life they were made to live. I highly recommend this book. It will not disappoint!"

MATT KELLER

Lead Pastor of Next Level Church, Fort Myers, Florida; author of God of the Underdogs

"Excitement, adventure, and success: These are things we pursue with reckless abandon. What can we conquer next? Conquest is good, but only if we're fully surrendered to God's plan. Rob Ketterling's new book, *Thrill Sequence*, will help you discover how to live a life of adventure in Christ."

CRAIG GROESCHEL

Senior Pastor of LifeChurch.tv; author of From This Day Forward: Five Commitments to Fail-Proof Your Marriage

"We were made to crave! We yearn for days of joy and excitement, for experiences and adventure. We want more but often don't know how to achieve a life beyond the mundane. In his inspiring new book, *Thrill Sequence*, Rob Ketterling provides the key to that full and daring life. The key is to possess a reckless faith. I encourage you to read this book and absorb the insightful teachings. Then spend the rest of your life living large with an authentic, audacious faith.

DR. DAVE MARTIN

America's #1 Christian Success Coach and author of Twelve Traits of the Greats

"Thrills are fun but fleeting. In his book *Thrill Sequence*, Rob challenges his readers to grab ahold of a reckless faith that follows Jesus into a life of eternal significance and fulfillment. Let Rob be your tour guide on the adventure of a lifetime!"

TODD MULLINS

Lead Pastor, Christ Fellowship, Palm Beach, Florida

"In his book *Thrill Sequence*, Rob Ketterling helps his readers move beyond temporary pleasures to the only thing that brings ultimate satisfaction!"

JOHN LINDELL

Lead Pastor, James River Assembly, Springfield, Missouri

THRILL SEQUENCE

LIVING FOR WHAT REALLY MATTERS

rob ketterling

SALUBRIS℠
RESOURCES

Published by Salubris Resources
1445 N. Boonville Ave.
Springfield, Missouri 65802

Cover design by PlainJoe Studios (www.plainjoestudios.com)
Interior formatting by Prodigy Pixel (www.prodigypixel.com)

ISBN: 978-1-68067-018-9

18 17 16 15 ● 1 2 3 4
Printed in the United States of America

This book is dedicated to my wife, Becca, and my boys, Connor and Logan. Being a husband and a father is the best and most rewarding thrill I've ever been on!

"You're addicted to thrills? What an empty life! The pursuit of pleasure is never satisfied."

PROVERBS 21:17 (THE MESSAGE)

CONTENTS

THE NEW CURRENCY OF CULTURE

"Money was never a big motivation for me, except as a way to keep score. The real excitement is playing the game."[1]

—DONALD TRUMP

YOU MIGHT REMEMBER motorcycle daredevil, Evel Knievel—or maybe your parents do! If you have no clue, Google him. He made a living attempting motorcycle jumps over just about everything—fountains, busses, even the Snake River Canyon. (I remember watching that on TV; he used a rocket—not his usual motorcycle—and it didn't go well!)

He suffered more than 433 bone breaks or fractures, earning him the dubious distinction of being placed in the *Guinness Book of*

---

1   BrainyQuote, posted at http://www.brainyquote.com/quotes/quotes/d/donaldtrum153802.html.

World Records for surviving the most broken bones. He also is the first guy to use social media (the TV) to brag about his experiences.

Knievel began his career working in a coal mine and eventually earned a promotion to the above-ground operation. He was fired from that job, however, for doing a "wheelie" with a large earthmover. The accident knocked out power for several hours in the city of Butte, Montana. He was a rodeo rider, ski jumper, and pole vaulter. He had run-ins with police and was even arrested for reckless driving after crashing his motorcycle.[2]

Knievel went on to make a career out of thrill seeking. He became an entertainment icon and was regularly featured on television, attempting to break records he previously set. The desire that drove Evel Knievel to risk his life in dangerous feats is the same drive that causes people to put their lives on the line today.

People love the attention their activities bring. The adrenaline rush is intoxicating and addictive. They can't stop. This is what I call the *thrill sequence*. I coined the term to describe the vicious cycle that culture embraces. People are searching for the next adventure and the thrills that come with it.

THE EVEL WITHIN

What is thrill sequence? In doing life, people get bored. They don't like being bored, so they go looking for a thrill. They experience the thrill and then share it with the world through various social media. Online "friends" venerate the bravery or audacity of the action. Then, the excitement wears off, and they get bored again. The cycle starts over, except this time the thrill must be bigger and better.

---

2   Wikipedia, "Evel Knievel," posted at http://en.wikipedia.org/wiki/ Evel_Knievel.

Has any culture ever been more obsessed with thrills than ours? From jumping off skyscrapers to pushing the limits of speed and endurance, and even designer kidnappings, people are in search of their next "wow that was awesome!" moment. Similar to Evel Knievel, they are willing to do anything to get it. We even make corn exciting in America with corn mazes that bring thrills to a cornfield near you! We are thrill seekers!

We pride ourselves on being able to find the next thrill in the most unusual and outlandish places. I've known people who have spent the majority of their lives searching for the next thrill—and it was their life plan all along. "I was there" and "I did it" are the currency they spend in every conversation as they try to one-up each other.

The daredevil approach to life isn't without its dangers. Sometimes, tragedy is the only evidence that a person went too far as they hang above a canyon or tried a "harmless" drug "just once." No matter what danger they face, some people just can't stop seeking the feeling that comes in pursuit of the next thrill. The adrenaline rush is addictive and powerful; it pushes them to new heights, new spaces, new challenges, and new opportunities again and again.

So what happens when the thrill stops being thrilling?

The law of diminishing returns helps define where the constant pursuit of a thrill begins to break down. It states:

> When increasing amounts of one factor of production are employed in production along with a fixed amount of some other production factor, after some point, the resulting increases in output of product become smaller and smaller.[3]

---

[3]   Paul M. Johnson, "Diminishing Returns, Law of," *A Glossary of Political Economy Terms*, posted at http://www.auburn.edu/~johnspm/gloss/diminishing_returns_law_of.

What does that mean? It means that, over time, people eventually have to work harder to achieve their desired thrill level. What thrilled them in the past won't thrill them in the future because they have already "been there, done that." It takes more and more effort to achieve an increased sense of accomplishment, and they start running out of ideas.

The search for the next thrill doesn't just show up among the young and adventurous; it shows up in almost every walk of life. People make decisions based on the perceived thrill and the promised rush. If something looks thrilling, they are in. If no thrill seems possible, there better be some exclusive bragging rights, or they'll find something else to do. They need bigger, faster, more spectacular, more daring adventures—another rush of adrenaline. All the while, they put themselves in danger personally, relationally, financially, and even spiritually.

Some people engage in criminal activity because of the thrill. How else do you explain rich kids stealing when they have money in their pockets? Others needlessly put their lives at risk. It can be an insatiable cycle of dangerous activity that points toward a personal tragedy. Some suffer permanent injury. Some lose their freedom. Some even lose their lives—all due to the pursuit of the next big thrill. It can be hard to escape the cycle because once you're in it, the momentary rush satisfies only until you need the next rush, and the next rush has to be bigger.

THRILLS ALL AROUND

The thrill sequence affects every area of life. People exchange their best possible lives for momentary thrills. It has become an epidemic. We have lost our bearings and flail around without direction or hope.

Our present is filled with options and our futures are uncertain, so we try to pack everything we can into the *now*. The thrill sequence always says, "More," but it never says, "Well done." Instead, it says, "What's next?" And all the while, it wears you out and steals your true joy. The 1991 movie *Point Break* gave us the term "adrenaline junkie," and people caught up in the thrill sequence know what it's like to be an adrenaline junkie.

A few years ago, someone coined the expression "experience cramming" to describe how people pack their experiences into online space by posting comments, pictures, videos, and blogs. Each new event provides the stepping stone to a bigger, more impressive event, and the more events, the better the cramming.

The expression "experience cramming" might be new, but the idea has been around for a long time. Today it reaches a new level of speed as we are more connected to one another's activities than ever before. In a world where people live out their lives online, telling the stories of their escapades can provide a sense of accomplishment. Many people try to outdo their friends, acquaintances, and even strangers with these experiences by being the first to post their phenomenal feats. Though some view this as entertaining—and some of it is meaningless fun—it has dangerous potential.

People can easily become infatuated with the popularity these thrills bring. They realize they must keep posting new thrills, or their status will fade. So off they go, becoming more daring and dangerous just to impress people they don't even know. The thrill is momentary. It never delivers what it promises. It can't satisfy the cravings they have for meaning and significance; yet they keep on cramming.

You would think we would realize that these momentary thrills don't deliver the long-lasting exhilaration people really want. We all need to step back and take a serious look at where we are in life and ask ourselves: Are we living up to our potential, or are we settling for something much less? We tell stories of our thrill sequence events with great inaccuracies, perhaps because lying is a byproduct of living for the thrills—cheap thrills versus meaningful experiences.

THRILL NOT THYSELF

My heart's desire is to let people know that God has a thrilling life in store for them. People who seek thrills aren't looking to the church for their next activity, and I can't say I blame them. Unfortunately, we have allowed the most thrilling experience in history—a relationship with God—to look boring, uninspiring, and anything but thrilling. There is nothing more invigorating than walking with Jesus day after day, but that's not how the world sees it.

Our gatherings might show signs of life, but our lives don't suggest we are thrilled with the journey. We may be thrilled with lots of things but, sadly, we are not so excited about the most significant thing. Compared to everything else in life that looks thrilling, most people's spiritual lives appear lacking.

The spiritual journey often begins with a thrill. New believers are excited and actively engaged in opportunities to learn and grow because, after all, they've just connected with the divine; they've connected with God. For a moment, they experience the thrill sequence, a *spiritual* thrill sequence. Initially, this thrill sequence is exhilarating and way outside of the ordinary. Then, however, many people grow complacent, inactive, and bored. Nothing about their spiritual lives says they are growing. Nothing looks thrilling.

This book will help those who don't believe in God to recognize the folly of seeking thrills that don't really matter. It will also challenge you to step out of the safe zone of mediocrity and self-gratification and into the abundant life Jesus promised. It will give meaning to your everyday life and your experiences; it will help you not to waste your adrenaline!

Who should read this book? It's for the person trapped in the thrill sequence and looking for an explanation or exit from the ride. It's for the person who is self-destructing in the thrill sequence. It's for anyone living for the next thrill but living without the thrill of knowing Jesus as Savior. It's for believers who have lost their passion for following Christ. It's for the church leader or pastor who needs to be reminded that serving God is an intense thrill if done right. It's for those who are disillusioned with faith, religion, or the church. This book is for anyone who wants to invest their life in something that never stops delivering satisfaction and fulfillment, for the restless person on a search for meaning and significance. In other words, this book is for everyone! It's for thrill seekers young and old!

What might happen if we refocused our culture's conversation around the adventure of following Jesus? Could it be that many people don't find following Him appealing because they know too many people who claim to be followers but live bland lives? I think it's time to reverse the trend and give today's thrill seekers something to consider.

THE JESUS ADVENTURE

Your life doesn't have to be boring, and neither does your relationship with God. He didn't set you on earth to occupy space. You are here intentionally. God decided you should be right here, right now. You are important to Him. You matter, and you have work to do, so why waste your adrenaline on things that won't matter when life is over?

What is the thing that you can't *not* do? Read that question again, very slowly. How can that rhythm of your heart be turned into something that makes a difference? It just might be that the greatest thrill of your life is behind an unopened door—the door that says, "I was born for this!"

I don't want you simply to read this book and then set it aside. I want to inspire you to go to a place you've never been before. God might want you to go on a mission trip or invest your skills in a local ministry that will change the lives of people who need hope. It should inspire you to share your faith by coming alive in ways that inspire others to ask you about your secret. In the pages that follow, you will be challenged to give of your time, talents, and resources in ways you might never have considered. You'll discover huge thrills as you take risks for God.

What's stopping you from living up to your God-given potential? Whatever the obstacles, we are going to address them through the power and wisdom of God's Word. God has a thrill sequence designed for everyone who will *really* follow Him. Any other thrills are cheap amusement park rides compared to the trip of a lifetime.

At the end of chapter 9 in the gospel of Luke, Jesus had brief encounters with three different men. His interactions with them provide the background for a significant life principle. Each man said he wanted to follow Jesus, but each wanted to do it in his own way. Each wanted to personalize the experience.

In many Bibles, the heading before Luke 9:57 is "The Cost of Following Jesus." There are two key words in that phrase: *cost* and *following*. When we investigate these terms, we discover that our typical understanding of "cost" and "following" is different from the meanings communicated in this passage.

We usually equate cost with money. So when we ask what it costs to follow Jesus, someone might think in terms of paying for something. In the Bible, the cost of following Jesus has nothing to do with money and everything to do with living up to His expectations.

Following someone is a matter of personal preference for some people. They follow as long as they are led where they want to go. Although that's the way many people live their spiritual lives, it isn't what Jesus expected. He expected total commitment. He presumed people would reorder their priorities so their commitment to Him was at the top of the list every day of the week. Jesus never called anyone to a one-day-per-week-when-it's-convenient spiritual life. He called them to a life of obedience and to the right kind of experience cramming.

With that in mind, here's what the first man in Luke 9:57 said, "I will follow you wherever you go." We aren't sure who the man was or how much of Jesus' teachings he had heard. His statement, however, sounds impressive. Yet a thorough examination of his words reveals a significant truth: There's a huge difference between a decision and a commitment. We can read a lot into the man's statement. Even though we might be confused about what he meant, we can be certain Jesus understood perfectly. In verse 58, Jesus basically said, "If you're following Me because of the personal benefit you'll receive, you don't understand what it means to follow Me." Within Jesus' words, we see a truth that is consistent throughout Scripture: There is no room for spectators in God's family. Those who follow Jesus do so on *His* terms.

Following Jesus is the authentic thrill sequence. As we follow Him, we learn more about who He wants us to be. We find our greatest significance when we set aside what we want out of life and focus on what He wants for us. He designed us. Shouldn't His plan be the best plan? Though we understand that reality, we find it difficult to live out. We struggle to set aside our personal agendas and plans. We like to chart our courses and invite God to come along for the journey, but that's not how God works.

Your friends aren't going to be bothered if you don't live up to God's potential for your life. As a matter of fact, they might discourage you from doing anything other than what you are doing right now. But they aren't accountable to God for your life—you are. One day, He will ask you to explain what you did with the life He entrusted to you. Are you living in preparation for that opportunity?

I'm delighted you decided to come along on this journey. This is the thrill sequence you never knew existed. It's God's plan for your best life, and trust me, it's thrilling! It's the ultimate thrill sequence!

chapter one

EXPERIENCE CRAMMING

"A man who carries a cat by the tail learns something he can learn in no other way."[4]

—MARK TWAIN

SOME PEOPLE BELIEVE we are defined by what we do. Since no one wants to live with a boring reputation, people often feel compelled to engage in ever-increasing activity with hopes of gaining some degree of superiority.

Dr. Frank Farley, the Laura H. Carnell Professor of Educational Psychology at Temple University, has labeled people in our culture as "T-types." They are in it for the thrill—the risk, the stimulation, the change, the variety, the intensity. These people are comfortable with uncertain outcomes. They are willing to take risks and live with the consequences. They are the new Evel Knievels, and there is not just

---

4   BrainyQuote, posted at http://www.brainyquote.com/quotes/quotes/m/marktwain105031.html.

one of them or a few of them. There are millions of them with varying degrees of desire.

CHRONIC THRILLDOM

Social media has popularized this lifestyle. Rather than write about their experiences, people now post pictures of whatever they are doing. Their lives are a dynamic online album instantaneously available to the world. This fuels the competitive nature so many people possess. Now we can compete across the globe, not just across the street.

As a culture, we are sucked into the vortex of incessant, sometimes unnecessary, activity. People cram as much activity as possible into their lives in an effort to achieve a desired level of significance. If you can't do it first, can you do more? That's what people are eagerly trying to live out—but there's a problem. The system they believe can produce personal significance can't deliver on its promises.

People want to feel rich, even if their riches are only contained in their experiences. They want to outdo others and are willing to do most anything for the distinction of being labeled "the best" or "the most extreme" or "the first."

In We Are All Weird, Seth Godin says:

> RICH is my word for someone who can afford to make choices, who has enough resources to do more than merely survive. . . . The swami I met in a small village in India is rich. Not because he has a fancy car (he doesn't). He's rich because he can make an impact on his tribe. Not just choices about what to buy, but choices about how to live.[5]

---

5   Seth Godin, We Are All Weird, Kindle version, (The Domino Project, 2011), location 70 of 1005.

We have the opportunity to choose how to live. Therefore, we are all rich. In Luke 12:48, Jesus said, "From everyone who has been given much, much will be demanded; and from the one who has been entrusted

We are accountable for more than our own self-gratification and accomplishments.

with much, much more will be asked." We have been entrusted with a lot. We are accountable for more than our own self-gratification and accomplishments. God expects much from us.

In *The Message*, Proverbs 21:17 says, "You're addicted to thrills? What an empty life! The pursuit of pleasure is never satisfied." The first time I read that, it jumped off the page because that's the thrill sequence! People who run this race will never be satisfied. This isn't how to find a meaningful life. This is a futile existence that's never satisfied.

Pastor John Piper said, "America is the first culture in jeopardy of amusing itself to death."[6] We have so much, we are so rich, but we are so dissatisfied with the quality of our lives. Ultimately, this cycle leads to chronic boredom because we run out of superlative experiences. The next thrill doesn't exceed the last thrill, so we settle into mediocrity or up the thrills to destructive behaviors that steal our lives away. It's hard to believe that people who have so much can lose what matters most because we are addicted to thrills.

DIE ALIVE

You don't have to die dull. You don't have to live beneath your potential. There's a way to find significance apart from the way the world thinks it can be found. If what everyone else is doing works,

---

6   John Piper, *Don't Waste Your Life*, quote posted at https://www.goodreads.com/work/quotes/247323-don-t-waste-your-life

why are there so many dissatisfied people? The world's plan *doesn't* work. Living for the next big thing leads to emptiness, yet we keep trying to find fulfillment in an empty promise.

Why is this concept so hard to grasp? Why do people continue to do something that doesn't have a track record for success? If you keep doing what you have always done, you will experience results you have already experienced. The future is predictable if your actions are consistent. I think most people would agree with that statement—it isn't the most profound thing you have heard. However, people continue to repeat the same cycles that landed them in their present state of dissatisfaction. This is humanity's folly. The Bible tells the stories of people who tried to do life their way, suffered the consequences of poor choices, and then repeated their pasts.

Perhaps you are familiar with the Bible story in the book of Exodus about the Israelites and their escape from slavery in Egypt. At the time, the distance from Egypt to Canaan could have been traveled in approximately three weeks with normal effort. However, the Israelites didn't take the most direct path. God led them a different way because they weren't ready to face the giants in their way, the Philistines. God's plan, however, was complicated by the nation's persistent disobedience. Time after time, they took matters into their own hands and made decisions that lengthened their journey—and three weeks turned into forty years. Their recipe for success never worked, but they kept doing what they had always done.

You can make your life have more meaning and purpose.

It sounds familiar, doesn't it? We have the same tendencies. Our recipes for success and fulfillment have failed, yet we keep trying them. Meanwhile, the clock ticks, and the calendar pages flip. Car seats give way to driving lessons and first dates. Our babies become adults who have babies who become adults. And each of us is left with a haunting question: What did I do with my life? Did my experiences even matter?

The time to answer that question isn't later; the time is right now. You can make your life have more meaning and purpose. You can choose a different path. In *A Whole New Mind*, Daniel Pink says:

> The paradox of prosperity is that while living standards have risen steadily decade after decade, personal, family, and life satisfaction haven't budged. That's why more people—liberated by prosperity but not fulfilled by it—are resolving the paradox by searching for meaning."[7]

People today think the next thrill will resolve the paradox.

What happened that made people believe busyness would produce fulfillment? Did a switch flip a few years ago, or has this been a gradual process? It didn't happen overnight. Our culture has been building toward this for decades. We have come to believe that one more activity on the schedule or one more organization on the agenda will bring fulfillment. When that activity or organization fails to deliver, we add more and more. Today, our children often participate in activities they don't even like. Parents have become taxi drivers and scheduling experts as they manage their children's busy lives. Why? It's not because the kids want the activities. It's because their parents are seeking significance vicariously through them. When parents can't add anything more to their lives, they add to their kids' lives. Can you relate?

---

7   Daniel Pink, *A Whole New Mind* (New York: Riverhead Trade, 2006), 35.

THE NEW "FINE, THANK YOU"

Busyness is the new status symbol for many people. Ask, "How are you doing?" and you might get, "It's been a busy week," in response. We get a similar answer when we ask how someone's week has been, what's on their schedule, how their kids are doing, and what do the next four months look like?

About fifty years ago, someone predicted that ours would be a more leisurely generation. Work weeks would shorten as automation eliminated repetitive activities. People would be more relaxed and at peace. Families would dine together at home. Kids would be kids. So much for predictions, huh?

Today, people are trying to outwork their competition. Our media connected society means we are always online. We believe we can multitask, in spite of research that shows multitasking is impossible. We eat in our cars (on average, Americans now eat one of five meals in their cars because they're so busy[8]) or meet in restaurants that double as playgrounds. Our kids have a soccer shoe on one foot and a ballet slipper on the other, with piano music in the right hand and a science project in the left. Some schools assign homework over the summer that must be submitted when school resumes in the fall. Life is more hectic than ever, and it shows no sign of letting up.

Busyness has a co-conspirator named *amusement*. The breakneck pace of everyday life makes people feel entitled to amusement. They live lives they can't wait to escape. Is that a recipe for fulfillment? There's a new trend in our culture. Many people in midlife are taking a closer look at the trajectories they are on and choosing to reorient their lives toward something more significant.

---

8   "11 Facts about American Eating Habits," DoSomething.org, posted at https://www.dosomething.org/facts/11-facts-about-american-eating-habits

They are walking away from things they once thought would give them meaning and significance. They have decided the pursuit of pleasure and things is a meaningless journey.

"The pursuit of pleasure is never satisfied" (Proverbs 21:17 MSG). *Pleasure* comes from the Hebrew word meaning *mirth*. That's not a word we use every day. It means *amusement*. No culture has been more fascinated with amusement than ours. According to the International Association of Amusement Parks and Attractions, there are more than four hundred amusement parks in America. Twenty-eight percent of Americans say they would be interested in working at an amusement park. (It's not necessarily a bad idea; I actually worked at one for three years and had a lot of fun doing it!) Amusement parks take in more than $12 billion per year.[9] Amusement is big business.

Yet amusement is designed to give life flavor, not to be the focus of life. When we give ourselves over to the pursuit of amusement, we compromise our true potential. God didn't design us to play our lives away. That message, unfortunately, has been drowned out in today's society. People still seek satisfaction through amusement, in

> God didn't design us to play our lives away.

spite of the fact that the Bible says seeking amusement will never lead to satisfaction. There will always be a bigger, faster rollercoaster or a new character-themed ride. People will find creative ways to rationalize spending lots of money on things guaranteed to provide momentary entertainment but no satisfaction.

What gives people pleasure today might not provide the same thrill tomorrow. Just look at the change that takes place each week in the technology industry. Accomplishments celebrated thirty years ago are laughable today. Mobile phones were once the size of a

---

9   IAAPA website, posted at http://www.iaapa.org/resources/by-park-type/ amusement-parks-and-attractions/industry-statistics#sthash.ua5uzUpv.dpuf.

lunch box. Calculators could only add, subtract, multiply, and divide, and they cost a lot of money. Remote controls were unheard of. The technology that amazed our parents is now commonplace in many Third World countries. But the technology world isn't letting up. The devices we use each day are obsolete in the minds of the people who designed them. They were already working on a replacement before my phone hit the market. Recently, Apple sold more iPhone 6 models than any other multi-million-selling iPhone in the company's stellar product sales history—39 *million* units in its first month[10]—even though most of those buyers already had an iPhone!

WHEN MORE ISN'T MORE

We follow a similar pattern of thinking to the technology industry. Whatever brings us joy today has the potential to be boring tomorrow. We want more, and tomorrow, we will want even more. What's the harm in wanting more? It's a dangerous cycle.

Let's say you decide to jump from a height of one foot today and then add one foot each subsequent day. The one-foot jump is more like a step. Two feet presents no problem. How will you know when jumping from a height is dangerous? You won't until you jump and hurt yourself. That's when you will decide you should have stopped one jump sooner.

The pursuit of pleasure is powerful. We push the limits, hoping to get a bigger thrill than the last. But we never know we've gone too far until we suffer the negative consequences. The Internet is loaded with stories and videos about people who pushed the limits and lost. Some simply got hurt. Others experienced more tragic results.

---

10   Hayley Tsukayama, "Apple Crushes Expectations, Sells 39.3 Million iPhones in Fourth Quarter," *The Washington Post*, posted at http://www.washingtonpost. com/blogs/the-switch/wp/2014/10/20/apple-crushes-expectations-sells-39-3-million-iphones-in-fourth-quarter/

Although "the pursuit of pleasure is never satisfied," the pursuit of God always satisfies. Everything entrusted to you—time, ability, money, influence, personality—was given to you by a loving Creator who has an assignment for you.

A youth Bible study teacher pulled a one hundred-dollar bill from his pocket and handed it to one of his students. He instructed the student to place the money in the offering basket during worship. The following week, the teacher asked the student what he did with the money. The student replied that he had put it in the offering. The teacher asked why he did that, and the student said, "It wasn't mine. It belonged to you, so I did what you said."

Your life and everything you have is like that one hundred-dollar bill, and you are the student. God handed it to you with instructions. You get to choose to do what He said or to take possession of something that isn't yours. Don't try to cram experiences into your life and, while doing so, miss out on what life is all about. It's not about the experiences; it's not about the thrill. There's much more to life than that. So don't settle for just doing something different. Do something more, and discover the One who can thrill you!

KEY IDEAS

- The "thrill sequence" describes the vicious cycle of continuously searching for the next adventure and the thrills that come with it.

- Social media has helped popularize the thrill sequence. Rather than write about their experiences, people now post pictures of whatever they are doing.

- There's a way to find significance apart from the way the world thinks it can be found.

- Busyness is the new status symbol for many people.

- Everything entrusted to you—time, ability, money, influence, personality—was given to you by a loving Creator who has an assignment for you.

DISCUSSION QUESTIONS

1. Take a close look at the definition of "thrill sequence," and describe how your life is affected by it.

2. What information do you share on social media, and why do you share it?

3. What makes you significant? What is your strategy for finding significance in life? How effective has your previous strategy been?

4. Describe a day in your life. How does busyness affect your ability to hear from God?

5. What do you think is God's assignment for you? How well can you know your God-given assignment without an intimate relationship with God?

ACTION STEPS

1. Get a journal or use an online journal to keep track of your activities for a week. Look for clues related to your focus in life.

2. Identify one activity you can eliminate from your schedule so you can spend more time with God. Ask Him to help you understand His assignment for your life.

chapter two

WHAT'S MISSING?

"I think there is a part of life that I'm missing."[11]

—KENNY CHESNEY (COUNTRY MUSIC SINGER)

YOU HAVE TO APPRECIATE the honesty of someone the world thinks has everything. In 2014, Chesney earned $44 million, enough for third place among country music stars, behind Toby Keith and Taylor Swift.[12] You would think Chesney had a great life. He has money, popularity, and can buy anything he wants. Yet, by his own admission, something is missing.

---

11   BrainyQuote, posted at http://www.brainyquote.com/quotes/quotes/k/
      kennychesn448278.html.

12   Zack O'Malley Greenburg, "Country Cash Kings 2014: Analysis
      and Aftermath," *Forbes*, posted at http://www.forbes.com/sites/
      zackomalleygreenburg/2014/08/04/country-cash-kings-2014-analysis-
      aftermath/.

A HOLE IN (EACH) ONE

Most of us would say we wish our lives were that "empty." But Chesney's comment reflects a condition that threatens every person on the planet. It's the futility generated by filling our lives with something other than the one thing we were designed for. Philosopher Blaise Pascal said it this way:

> What else does this craving, and this helplessness, proclaim but that there was once in man a true happiness, of which all that now remains is the empty print and trace? This he tries in vain to fill with everything around him, seeking in things that are not there the help he cannot find in those that are, though none can help, since this infinite abyss can be filled only with an infinite and immutable object; in other words by God himself.[13]

In short, Pascal said our emptiness can only be filled by God . . . period. Chase all the thrills you want, but it all comes back to God.

Many people agree in theory with Pascal and others believe fulfillment can only be found in relationship with our Creator. Practically speaking, however, there is a disconnect between theory and reality in their lives. People have substituted representations of God for God Himself. They have tried religion, religious activity, and religious leadership, all to no avail. Some might argue that fulfillment can't be found this side of heaven. Certainly, the eternal experience will supersede anything we know, but our existence here

---

13   Blaise Pascal, Pensees, cited in Douglas Groothuis, "Incorrect Pascal Quotes," The Constructive Curmudgeon blogsite, posted at http:// theconstructivecurmudgeon.blogspot.com/2006/05/incorrect-pascal-quotes. html.

and now can be more fulfilling than most people realize. If you don't know heaven is waiting for you, you try to squeeze all you can out of this life. The problem is, you can't squeeze the joy you're looking for out of this life because it's just not there.

How many people go through life thinking something is missing? They suffer from FOMO—fear of missing out. Are you one of them? Chances are good that you have had that thought, are having

Chase all the thrills you want, but it all comes back to God.

that thought, or will have it in the future. It's a common perplexity of the human race. Unlike social media, this condition has been around for a long time. It dates way back to the beginning of time, to Genesis, to a garden and a man and a woman.

You might know the story. God created the world and then created man and placed him in the garden of Eden. There, the man had everything he wanted, and the place was governed by only one rule: stay away from the tree in the middle of the garden. Simple, right? Wouldn't life be great if there were only one rule?

Because the man was lonely—after all, the only companions he had were animals—God created the woman. The same rule that applied to the man applied to her. She was free to enjoy the garden as long as she stayed away from the tree in the middle of the garden. So far, so good.

We don't know how much time the man and woman spent being totally satisfied by everything God provided. It might have been days, years, or decades, although I doubt it was decades! Eventually, however, temptation came calling in the form of a serpent. The serpent's conversation with the woman changed the course of history. He called God's motives into question and made the woman believe God was hiding something from her. He persuaded her that

God's plan wasn't the best plan for her life and that there were greater thrills to be discovered.

The remainder of the story is familiar: The man and woman ate from the tree and realized that doing things their way didn't deliver the fulfillment they sought. They discovered the tragedy of disappointing God and tried to hide. They made excuses. They got kicked out of the garden, and the thrill sequence was born.

Outside the garden, life didn't get better. One of their sons killed the other. Life spiraled out of control. Could all of this chaos really be connected to that one situation when they ate from the tree God prohibited? Yes. That's exactly what happened. They fell into the trap of thinking life's ultimate satisfaction could be found apart from God's principles and rules. They discovered the hard way that they were wrong.

> We can't find our true happiness outside of God, so why do we keep chasing the thrills and experiences?

The tragic events found in the opening pages of the Bible have been repeated throughout history. People have never stopped believing they could create a better life than the life made available through a relationship with God. No one has ever succeeded, but people still try. St. Augustine saw that "we look for happiness, not in You, but in what You have created." We can't find our true happiness outside of God, so why do we keep chasing the thrills and experiences?

PREDICTABLE FOOLS

We need to take a critical look at the thrill sequence to see if there's something more worth living for. Is there something more important? I believe there is. Proverbs 15:21 says, "The empty-headed treat life as a play thing. The perceptive grasp its meaning and make a go of it"

(*The Message*). The New International Version puts it this way: "Folly brings joy to one who has no sense, but whoever has understanding keeps a straight course."

Do you see the distinction between the empty-headed and the perceptive? Which one are you? Which one do you want to be? Before you answer, take a moment to think about your activities over the past week or two. Check your social media accounts. Does your life support what your mouth says?

Few people go through life planning to be empty-headed. There may be some on reality television shows, but that's *not* reality. For the rest of us, we don't want to be viewed as people who have no sense. However, when we treat life as a plaything, the Bible is right: we declare our foolishness. What's the other option? We need to be perceptive. The dictionary defines *perceptive* as "having or showing keenness of insight, understanding, or intuition."[14]

There is a lot of life we can't predict, but some choices have predictable consequences. If you eat more calories than you burn, you'll gain weight. That's a proven fact. It's predictable. If you don't save money, Christmas might be a challenge. Christmas falls on December 25 every year. It's predictable. We should never get to mid-December and say, "Oh, my goodness, Christmas is coming. I never expected that."

God also gives you intuition—direct perception of truth. Sometimes you get a feeling that something isn't right. You feel as if a specific decision might have unfavorable consequences. You don't have proof or data; you just know. God uses intuition to guide us. He doesn't want us to make mistakes. He prompts us through the Holy Spirit.

---

14   Dictionary.com, "perceptive," posted at http://dictionary.reference.com/browse/perceptive

The more we tune in to God's guidance, the more meaning our lives will have. Why do multimillionaires still search for meaning? Some aren't in the habit of tuning their lives to God's direction. Their wealth, success, experiences, and popularity leave them with a sense of emptiness. Although celebrated publicly, they face the possibility of doing something no one wants to do: they might die dull.

FILLED TO "EMPTY"

Like I said, you don't have to die dull. But living out the thrill sequence of the world's standards will take you there. So will watching television eighteen hours a day. Those are extremes that should be avoided. God has more for you to do.

Solomon, the son of David, was one of the wealthiest kings in the Bible. He was also the wisest. He inherited the responsibility of building the temple in Jerusalem. At the dedication of the temple, Solomon went before God to make a sacrifice. God told Solomon to ask for anything he wanted. Solomon asked for wisdom, and God gave it to him.

In the book of Ecclesiastes, we see Solomon's thoughts regarding the way people live. During his reign, people prospered. Life in Jerusalem and all of Israel was good. Yet he saw people living aimlessly. He saw them grow more consumed with busyness and less concerned about obedience. He saw something we see in our culture today.

Ecclesiastes 1:1 begins with Solomon identifying himself as the teacher, David's son. Then he makes a statement that wouldn't normally be used to hook readers and make them want to hang on for the rest of the story. He says, "Meaningless! Meaningless! Utterly meaningless! Everything is meaningless." Talk about jumping in with both feet!

These were the observations of a man who lived a life almost everyone envied. He had the best food, countless servants, unlimited resources, God-given wisdom, and more wives than he needed. But as he scanned the horizon and saw people busying themselves

> The more we tune in to God's guidance, the more meaning our lives will have.

with thrill after thrill, he realized the foolishness of their actions. They were busy but unfulfilled. They were winning, according to the world's definition of winning, but felt like losers. Life was full, but they were empty.

That's the beauty of the Bible. Though written long ago, its descriptions of culture are amazingly accurate today. I guess the saying is true: history repeats itself. Solomon saw what many people today experience. They have full schedules but empty lives. They have a collection of trophies but feel insignificant. Their lives look satisfying, but their demeanor tells a different story. Something is missing, but they don't know what it is. You can be winning but feel like a loser and look like you're full when you're empty.

Solomon's observations continue in Ecclesiastes 1:12,

I've been king over Israel in Jerusalem. I looked most carefully into everything, searched out all that is done on this earth. And let me tell you, there's not much to write home about. God hasn't made it easy for us. I've seen it all and it's nothing but smoke—smoke, and spitting into the wind. (*The Message*)

Solomon said he had looked over everything and decided "there wasn't much to write home about." His words might seem discouraging, but Solomon eventually made a point. Remember, he was the wisest man in the world!

He continued his thoughts in Ecclesiastes 2:1, "I said to myself, 'Let's go for it—experiment with pleasure, have a good time!' But there was nothing to it, nothing but smoke" (*The Message*). No one could experiment with pleasure like Solomon. His unlimited resources and authority meant that nothing was out of reach. He could try anything he wanted; he was the Richard Branson of his day and then some! The result, however, was the same. He came up empty. Pleasure didn't fill the void.

What did Solomon do in his search for meaning? He tells us in verses 4–10:

> Oh, I did great things: built houses, planted vineyards, designed gardens and parks and planted a variety of fruit trees in them, made pools of water to irrigate the groves of trees. I bought slaves, male and female, who had children, giving me even more slaves; then I acquired large herds and flocks, larger than any before me in Jerusalem. I piled up silver and gold, loot from kings and kingdoms. I gathered a chorus of singers to entertain me with song, and—most exquisite of all pleasures—voluptuous maidens for my bed. Oh, how I prospered! I left all my predecessors in Jerusalem far behind, left them behind in the dust. What's more, I kept a clear head through it all. Everything I wanted I took—I never said no to myself. I gave in to every impulse, held back nothing. I sucked the marrow of pleasure out of every task—my reward to myself for a hard day's work! (*The Message*)

Solomon tried everything. He was living the ultimate thrill sequence, and verse 11 begins his evaluation of his life:

Then I took a good look at everything I'd done, looked at all the sweat and hard work. But when I looked, I saw nothing but smoke. Smoke and spitting into the wind. There was nothing to any of it. Nothing. (*The Message*)

Look back at Solomon's list of accomplishments and pleasures. What didn't he do? How could he say it was nothing? Smoke and spit? Like many people today, he burned out. He entertained himself right into a funk that he couldn't escape. To him, his life was dumb. The wisest man on earth had a dumb life. How sad is that?

We can learn from Solomon because our lives are a lot like his. You might be burning the candle at both ends. You're running from activity to activity, sometimes forgetting to do things you know you should do. You might not have Solomon's riches, but you are living your own version of the thrill sequence. It's not working for you, and I bet it feels a lot like smoke and spit.

In chapter 2 of Ecclesiastes, Solomon used a first-person pronoun approximately sixty times, depending on the translation. He talked a lot about himself because that's what his life was all about. He used everything available to create a world that served him well. Yet his life was empty because a life of self is an empty life.

Solomon checked every box on his bucket list. He outdid every king before or after him. He was the record setter, trendsetter, and standard bearer for success. He had seven hundred wives and three hundred concubines. That's one thousand wives. If he spent a week with each one, it would take nineteen years to spend seven days with all of them! He could have a "Wife of the Day" and still not see the same wife for three years! He had any woman he wanted, and he never had to post a picture on an online dating site. One thousand wives . . . but he still lacked something.

DUMB HAPPENS

What's missing in the lives of people who have everything? Solomon recognized the truth. In Ecclesiastes 12:13–14, he said:

> The last and final word is this: Fear God. Do what he tells you. And that's it. Eventually God will bring everything that we do out into the open and judge it according to its hidden intent, whether it's good or evil. (*The Message*)

Fear God, and do what He tells you. (Fear of God is living in respect, awe, and submission to God, not trembling because of Him.) Fear of or submission to God is the missing ingredient. God designed you for a thrilling life, but His design doesn't give you permission to leave Him *out* of your life. The most thrilling life is found in the middle of God's plan. You find real peace and joy in relationship with God, not while running from Him and toward everything else.

> The most thrilling life is found in the middle of God's plan.

Let's go back to the Garden of Eden. After the man and woman ate from the forbidden tree, they made coverings for themselves and tried to hide from God. Who can hide from God's omniscient eyes? No one! But poor choices make people dumb. Adam and Eve made a bad choice and then did some dumb things.

It's easy to try to avoid the issue by settling into your dumbness. I'm not being critical, just honest. Dumbness is the state of being that results from trying to make life meaningful without a relationship with the One who gives life meaning.

At the end of your life, no one is going to care what car you drove, where you lived, hiked, or swam, where you ate or what you ate, or what near-death adventure you had. Those things will evaporate into the nothingness Solomon described unless they're attached to something deeper. What matters at the end of life is what God does with you, in you, and through you. If you live your earthly life in reverence and fear of God, you will love Him and be delighted in Him. You will want to obey Him.

You can live life out of balance because that's the way everyone else is doing it. If you don't know heaven is yours, you'll try to squeeze all you can out of this earth, but the joy you are looking for isn't found on this earth. God wants something more for you. He wants you to thrive while alive and join Him in heaven when this earthly life is over.

Is something missing for you?

KEY IDEAS

- Our emptiness can only be filled by God. Period.

- People have never stopped believing they can create a better life than the life made available through a relationship with God.

- The more we tune in to God's guidance in our lives, the more meaning our lives will have.

- You find real peace and joy in relationship with God, not while running from Him.

- God wants you to thrive while alive and join Him in heaven when this earthly life is over.

DISCUSSION QUESTIONS

1. What are some ways people try to fill their emptiness?
    What have you tried?

2. Why do people think they can create a better life apart
    from God than they can with God?

3. What is your practice for tuning in to God's guidance
    in your life?

4. In what ways does your relationship with God affect
    your peace and joy?

5. What would your life look like if you were thriving?

ACTION STEPS

1. Use your journal to identify some things that you do
    regularly. At the end of each day, take a few moments
    to rate each activity as positive or negative based on
    God's perspective.

2. Read through Ecclesiastes as if you had written it
    about your life. Write down what you learn or think
    through this process.

A BORING CHRISTIANITY

> "Hobbies of any kind are boring except to people who have the same hobby. This is also true of religion, although you will not find me saying so in print."[15]
>
> **—DAVE BARRY**

I REMEMBER THE first time I saw what you see on the cover of this book. It's called fly boarding, and it's the closest thing to feeling like a super hero most of us will ever feel. When I saw it, I immediately thought, "I need to do that!" (I still haven't, and my wife says I'm too old!) Fly boarding looks really cool, but there's a conflict going on in me as I consider it. I wonder, *Can a Christian really take the time to enjoy fly boarding—or any thrill of this world?* I get that a lot.

---

15   Thinkexist.com, posted at http://en.thinkexist.com/quotation/hobbies_of_
any_kind_are_boring_except_to_people/202590.html.

THRILLS FOR DINNER

As a pastor, a Christian, and an American, I know there are all sorts of opportunities for thrills and also all sorts of opportunities to meet needs. There's a pang of guilt in this tug of war, and we all have to ask, "Is it okay to live a thrilling life?" Notice I'm not just adding living a thrilling life "for God" as part of it. I'm wondering if we can really live *in* the thrill sequence world but not be *of* it. You know, like the apostle Paul said, "Do not be conformed to this world" (Romans 12:2 NKJV).

Does that include innocent fun? Does it mean no fly boarding? No golf? (I love golf, and it's my only hobby!) I believe bucket lists are okay and have one myself. I just encourage you to think like Ann Voskamp, author of *One Thousand Gifts,* and do an "empty myself" bucket list.

I know I need to abstain from things like adultery, drugs, and materialism, and trust me, that's part of the worldly thrill sequence we all should avoid. But fly boarding? Jet skiing? Golfing? Is it okay to enjoy a few thrills?

I have to say yes. I think we can enjoy them, but we need to make sure we are not thrilled by them. By that I mean living for them and hoping they will fulfill us. Here is what I have realized: these things—let me be clear, the innocent things—are meant to be dessert and never the main course. They're meant to fill your sweet tooth, not your stomach.

But is it possible to eat too much dessert? Of course it is. Look at the waist sizes of many people. In my first book, *Change Before You Have To,* I explained that losing weight changed my life because my problem was that dessert had become a main course. I ate three desserts a day—after breakfast, lunch, and dinner! So I cut out all desserts, lost the weight, and stabilized. Now I do a *taste* of dessert once in a while, not three times a day.

People sometimes come up to me if I'm eating a dessert and say, "I thought you changed; why are you eating dessert?"

"I changed, and I'm maintaining," I tell them. "Some dessert is okay. A taste is fine. Seriously, one cookie won't kill you."

So how do I know when a good thing has gone too far? I have a few checks. I weigh myself daily to see immediately if I'm out of balance. If I am, I hit the trails, eat the protein bars, eliminate the tastes of dessert, and get back in line.

My clothes also tell where I'm at. When I put on a shirt or pair of pants that should fit and they're tight, I put them back in the closet but let the moment speak to me. If the thing that should fit doesn't, I know I've been having too much of a good thing. This checkpoint reminds me of Romans 13:14: "Rather, clothe yourselves with the Lord Jesus Christ, and do not think about how to gratify the desires of the flesh." If your life doesn't "fit" what you should be wearing in Christ, it's probably because a good thing has become too much of a thing, or a bad thing has become the main thing. You need to stop and get your life in order so you fit a life clothed with the Lord.

> If your life doesn't "fit" what you should be wearing in Christ, it's probably because a good thing has become too much of a thing, or a bad thing has become the main thing.

How do you know if you're involved in an innocent thrill that can lead to a distracted life and not necessarily a destructive one? If it's frivolous or causes no friction in your life, the thrill is probably innocent. On the other hand, if it causes you to fight or could be fatal, it's most likely going to destroy you.

Another way to find out if a good thing has gone bad is to find a person who can be a mirror to you. Give this person permission to speak into your life about things they see that may be out of order. It could be a peer or a mentor, but the important thing is that you trust the person and they can be honest enough to tell you what you need to hear, so you don't get sucked into the thrill sequence.

What are *your* scales? What gives you instant feedback? What in your life is the mirror you consult? Think: frivolous, friction, fight, fatal. *Anything* that has the fatal label attached to it: run!

Adultery and drugs: run! Love of money: run, run, run! (This one can be hard to see; it's easy to think you're "just getting ahead.") Accumulating material possessions: run! Hold *things* loosely. Listen to God as He whispers what to give, keep, buy, or sell. And whatever you do: never make dessert the main course!

CHURCH NOW AND THEN

Ask people to describe some of their most boring experiences, and you'll probably hear someone talk about a time when they were in church. To some people, it seems that boredom and religion are synonymous. I understand. We have inadvertently made Christianity boring. Worse than that, we have almost made it a sort of punishment—I know that firsthand!

When I was a child, my parents brought my younger brother Rick and me to church. Being kids, we were curious, active, and not thrilled with pipe organs, hard wooden pews, or the idea of sitting still. We soon found out that climbing over the pews and distracting other people who looked like they enjoyed our entertainment more than the sermon led to smacks and even spankings. So, not wanting to receive either of those, I learned to be bored and find quiet ways to "amuse" myself at church. I used to look up at the lights or rub my eyes until this burned a dot in my vision when I blinked. Then I would simply blink and move this dot I was seeing all service long and amuse myself to avoid punishment. My view of church was that it was apparently necessary but boring.

There is a common misconception out there. Maybe you've heard it. Some people believe that living for anything other than thrills will be boring and dull. Specifically, they believe that if you live for God, your life will be boring and dull. How many people have you heard say, "I don't want to be just a Christian; I don't want to just go to heaven and strum a harp or something. I don't want to do that. It's boring and dull." This is a huge problem because they think Christianity is bland.

That's not the way Christianity began, and it's not how it's supposed to be lived today. In its early days, the Christian faith was lived out in a dynamic community that was far more than a weekend gathering. It was how people *did life*. We can gain some wisdom by taking a closer look at how things were when the church was new.

The New Testament church was born during tumultuous times. For three years, the community developed and grew as people followed the same person: Jesus. His death on the cross, however, removed the uniting figure and caused people to rethink the purpose of the church.

Peter's sermon at Pentecost brought people to a point of personal crisis. His explanation of the good news of Jesus' power over death challenged his audience to reconsider their lives and their relationships with God. He explained Jesus in a clear and concise way.

When the message of the gospel is clearly explained, people will respond. That happened in the first century when the Holy Spirit's arrival at Pentecost unleashed a wave of new believers. What would the faith community look like, and what would be its uniting factor? The early believers didn't want their faith to be boring. A boring faith isn't attractive to others.

At the end of Acts 2, excitement swelled within the faith community. Believers saw God's power at Pentecost. They heard Peter's sermon and witnessed its effects on the crowd. They had a ringside seat for God's demonstration of love, grace, mercy, and forgiveness. They had a lot to talk about! They weren't content to let hearing the sermon be their whole experience that day. Hearing the truth required personal action. They were thrilled with the message of the grace of God and used that energy to change the world! There's nothing boring about that!

> The early believers didn't want their faith to be boring. A boring faith isn't attractive to others.

Many people today are unmoved by an encounter with the truth of God's Word. They are distracted, confused, or lethargic about the significance of a personal relationship with God, but that's not the way it's supposed to be. Those who heard Peter's sermon didn't need to be persuaded to apply its truths to their lives; it came naturally.

Peter explained to the people how they could be saved from eternity in hell; he told them to repent and be baptized. This was great news to a group of people who had been made to feel like spiritual outsiders. They grew up thinking God was the property of the religious elite and now He could be theirs—or better yet, they could be His! The realization that God's love and forgiveness was available to all people was cause for celebration.

No one is beyond God's reach. His love extends to those who are close and to those who are far away. In the context of dynamic relationships with other believers, we can pray for our family members, friends, and acquaintances who don't know God, and watch what happens. Many people come to know Christ through the encouragement of impassioned believers, because deep within us all is a desire to find what we are created for and the One who created us.

Not everyone responded positively to Peter's message. That's why he continued to plead with them. Not only did he plead, but he also warned them. These were strong words. The crowd didn't realize Jerusalem would be destroyed about forty years later. They had no way of knowing they would be scattered throughout the land as a result of Rome's invasion. The point is this: We can't squander the opportunities we have to encourage people in their walk with

> Our investment in the lives of others gives our faith a true life purpose.

God. Our investment in the lives of others gives our faith a true life purpose. It's not only about what happens when we die; it's about how we live while on the earth.

The early church couldn't get enough fellowship. Believers met corporately in the temple, but they also met in homes to grow in relationships and to increase their knowledge of God's Word. The infant church suddenly had three thousand new believers who needed to be educated, trained, and encouraged in their walk with Christ.

> They devoted themselves to the apostles' teaching and to fellowship, to the breaking of bread and to prayer. Everyone was filled with awe at the many wonders and signs performed by the apostles. All the believers were together and had everything in common. They sold property and possessions to give to anyone who had need. Every day they continued to meet together in the temple courts. They broke bread in their homes and ate together with glad and sincere hearts, praising God and enjoying the favor of all the people. And the Lord added to their number daily those who were being saved. (Acts 2:42–47)

We see in these verses the biblical model for authentic community. The key word here is *devoted*. The New King James Version translates this as "continued steadfastly." (I really like that phrase!) The original Greek term suggests a steady commitment. This wasn't sporadic, irregular attendance. This was a new way to live life!

For the early believers, their relationship with God was at the center of their lives, and everything else wrapped around it. That's so different from many of today's Christians who set Jesus aside until they take Him out for special days. The early Christians did more than tolerate Bible study; they craved it. They saw spiritual value in spending time with other believers. Within their small groups, God did incredible things. As a result, their lifestyles were characterized by praise. God's work in their lives was on the tips of their tongues because God was renewing their minds and changing their lives. Their faith was contagious!

In Acts 2:47, we read that people continued to make Jesus their Savior and were added to the church. How did that happen? After all, the sermon was over, the congregation scattered, and yet the people stayed connected.

CONNECTIVE ISSUES

When people talk about their personal experiences with God, others are intrigued. Most people want a life that matters. They crave supportive, trusting relationships with people who are genuinely concerned about them. They want to be connected to the family of faith and to individuals within it, and that's how the early church grew.

What do I mean when I say the early believers were connected? The word *connect* doesn't appear in this text. However, the principles of connecting are obvious:

- *The early Christians connected physically*—they spent time together.

- *They connected philosophically*—they shared common beliefs and life principles.

- *They connected mentally and emotionally*—they were there for each other.

Specifically, the early church had some characteristics we should cultivate in our churches today. Let's take a look at a few desirable traits.

They were devoted. The word translated *devoted* is the Greek word *proskartereo*, which means steadfast commitment to a course of action. The early believers weren't committed to weekly attendance or financial support; they were committed to the mission of the movement. And because they were committed to the mission, they invested time and resources.

They studied the apostles' teaching. This refers to a small body of material considered authoritative because of its subject and source. The subject was the message about Jesus Christ. The source was authentic apostles. This body of material most likely contained some of Jesus' words and teachings (see Acts 20:35), an account of Jesus' life, ministry, and resurrection (Acts 2:22–24), and the practical application of Jesus' teaching to everyday life (1 Corinthians 15:3–5). This would become the *paradosis* (tradition); it would be passed from generation to generation. Throughout the New Testament, the role of teachers and the importance of teaching is reinforced.

They participated in the fellowship. Don't overlook the importance of the article *the*. There must have been something unique about the community of believers. The word for *fellowship* is the familiar Greek word *koinonia*. The fellowship of believers was distinct in that its members believed Jesus Christ was the Messiah. They were committed to sharing the redemptive message of hope with the world. The early believers apparently were effective because people were added to the fellowship daily. Evangelism in the early church wasn't a program; it was a lifestyle. Evangelism wasn't the responsibility of a few. It was the responsibility of everyone who called themselves a Christ-follower. That hasn't changed.

They took part in the breaking of bread. Was this an early Jewish fellowship meal, or was it more like our observance of the Lord's Supper? The arrangement of the words is significant. In context, it's unlikely that Luke would reference a simple meal or social gathering between two spiritually significant ideas, the community of believers and prayer. The breaking of bread must have been on par with the ideas that precede and follow its mention. This leads many theologians to conclude that Luke's reference was to a meal characterized by joy, love, and praise. It was around the table that people shared their stories. This, of course, created a fertile environment for the next thing on Luke's list.

They prayed together. Luke understood the importance of prayer in Jesus' life. In this verse, he points out that the early church also was dependent upon dynamic prayer.

When we put all of these elements together, we begin to understand the strength of the New Testament fellowship. People were connected to the mission and to those on the mission. This wasn't a passive, consumer-minded affiliation with an organization—this was life. Everything else flowed around it, and I bet it was thrilling to everyone involved!

First-century believers were Bible students. There is a direct connection between a person's Bible study habits and their spiritual vitality. People who browse the Bible can grow weary of their religious pursuits because they don't seem to be growing in their relationship with God. On the other hand, people who are serious students of God's Word continue to discover new truths from the most familiar passages. Even if you read the same thing over and over again you get something out of it. I like to say that the Bible has "time release" insights just waiting to be discovered the next time you read it!

When the community of faith does all of the things described above, great things happen. Let's look at what happened in the first century.

Everyone was filled with awe. Awe is defined as an overwhelming feeling of reverence, admiration, or fear, produced by that which is grand, sublime, extremely powerful, or the like. The people were in awe of two things: God and His movement among them. As they gathered in community they saw people who were transformed by God's power. They shared their stories. They celebrated God's goodness. They focused their lives on God. This is step one in the pursuit of a faith that matters.

> People who are serious students of God's Word continue to discover new truths from the most familiar passages.

They witnessed wonders and miraculous signs. Luke used terminology that he probably picked up from his study of the prophecy of Joel (Joel 2:19) and from Peter's sermon (Acts 2). Wonders and signs are tangible evidence of God's presence among believers. Luke wanted his readers to understand that Jesus performed miracles to assure people that He was God. The wonders and signs of the apostles were evidence of God's presence and power.

The believers were together and had all things in common. The first-century believers in Jerusalem shared a sense of spiritual unity that was strengthened by communal living. By living together in community, the believers knew the needs of others. Because they were sensitive to God's movement among them, they met needs as they arose and as God prompted them to help.

This was before the extreme persecution of Christians. However, early believers were probably subject to social and economic prejudices. At the time, this was true of any minority group. The communal life described in these verses was a survival tactic that had significant spiritual benefits. By living in community with other believers, needs were shared and met regularly.

They sold their property and possessions. Property (ktemata) referred to their real estate. Possessions (hyparxeis) were their personal belongings. Apparently, there was nothing the believers wouldn't sacrifice to meet the needs of others. They were living a thrill sequence of having less to do more, not doing more to have less! People in need were more important than personal possessions, animals, or real estate. These believers, however, weren't careless with their money or possessions. Because they were *doing life together,* they knew the needs were legitimate.

They met daily in the temple courts. The Jerusalem believers continued observing the Jewish customs and traditions. Their favorite place to meet was the temple at the eastern edge of the outer court. This area was called Solomon's Colonnade. At that place, they discussed their faith and offered praise to God. They didn't see themselves as a renegade religious sect; they were the faithful few who understood the Jewish Law and its prophecy of a Savior. This belief fueled the tensions between the Jews who didn't accept Jesus and those who did. The Christ-followers believed they were the true children of God and were willing to engage leaders of traditional Judaism in debates about Jesus and His deity, hoping to convince them.

They ate together in their homes. Though they worshiped at the temple, they ate meals in their homes. This is where their conversation turned from theological premises to practical application. Because they were focused on meeting the needs of others, they probably saw this as an opportunity to help those who didn't have access to adequate food. The word for food (*trophe*) suggests a substantial meal for which everyone was grateful.

FAITH LIKE JESUS

The Christian faith began with a viral enthusiasm that fueled the spread of the gospel. People came to faith in Christ because they saw the difference faith made in the lives of other people. Hope is contagious, and everyone is looking for it.

> Hope is contagious, and everyone is looking for it.

What has happened since those early days of enthusiasm? Could it be that people don't follow Jesus today because we have presented Him and the church as boring, predictable, and uninteresting? A once-a-week gathering and only-in-a-crisis-do-you-look-for-more kind of faith?

There's a difference between having a dynamic faith and being a member of an organization, but I fear we have lost that distinction. You might have left the church because you were bored. I want to encourage you to separate your perception of the church from your perception of Jesus. Jesus is never boring, though the church can be.

Jesus came to solve a problem religion couldn't solve. Religion can't erase your sin debt. It can't give you hope for the future. It will never sustain you when life caves in all around you. Jesus, however, has already paid for your sin. Because He is God, He offers hope for the future. His suffering qualifies Him to stand alongside you during difficult times.

John Ortberg said, "I hate how hard spiritual transformation is and how long it takes. I hate thinking about how many people have gone to church for decades and remain joyless or judgmental or bitter or superior."[16] I couldn't agree more with what he said, and I want you to know, it doesn't have to be that way! God hasn't changed. The dynamic faith we read about in the Bible is still possible in our lives today. We don't have to be bored. As a matter of fact, if you are bored in your relationship with God, it's most likely your fault.

God spoke the world into existence. He sent His Son to die for our sins but raised Him to life on the third day. He empowered the apostles, attracted followers, and offers hope. He is everything the Bible says He is.

He isn't boring, out of touch with reality, or unconcerned about your life. On the contrary, the most amazing life possible is available through a relationship with Him. It makes sense. The One who defines fulfillment offers it to those who love Him.

Don't fall into the habit of going through religious motions. Discover the thrill of living in a right relationship with God, and you'll discover a thrilling life. That's the antidote to a boring Christianity.

KEY IDEAS

- Some people believe that if you live for God, your life will be boring and dull.

- In its early days, the Christian faith was lived out in a dynamic community that was far more than a weekend gathering.

---

16   BrainyQuote, posted at http://www.brainyquote.com/quotes/quotes/j/johnortber526279.html#F5wr21DztSggDo8c.99.

- No one is beyond God's reach. His love extends to those who are close and to those who are far away.

- There is a direct connection between a person's Bible study habits and their spiritual vitality.

- The dynamic faith we read about in the Bible is still possible in our lives today.

DISCUSSION QUESTIONS

1. On a scale of one to ten with one being dull and ten being thrilling, rate your spiritual life. Explain why you gave it the rating you did.

2. In one sentence, describe the context of your faith. Where and how do you experience it?

3. Why is it hard for people to believe God's love extends to them?

4. What do your Bible study habits say about your spiritual vitality? What do you need to do to improve your spiritual vitality?

5. What are some things you need to do or to stop doing, so you can focus more on your personal spiritual growth?

6. Are you even on the path of spiritual growth? Where are you with respect to God's thrill sequence?

ACTION STEPS

1. Use your journal to log your "spiritual activity." Take note of the amount of time you spend with God as compared to the amount of time you spend on the Internet or using social media.

2. Look for ways to allow your relationship with God to be more influential in your life.

3. Take some time to reflect on your own moment of salvation. What first excited you about taking the step to follow God?

chapter four

JUNK FOOD FAITH

"Everyone would be healthier if they didn't eat junk food."[17]

—ROBERT ATKINS

HAVE YOU EVER been so hungry you ate junk food? I know I have. Recently, while on a road trip with my wife, our flight was cancelled due to thunderstorms. This meant the only way to get home was to rent a car and drive three hours to Kansas City. One hour in, we made a pit stop and hit the junk food like we were college students, except we are twenty years removed from college! We grabbed Red Bull, Diet Dr. Pepper, Sour Patch Kids, licorice, beef jerky, chips, and a protein bar or two. The junk food started to "speak" to me on the rest of our trip and well into the night. I know now that my body doesn't

---

17   BrainyQuote, posted at http://www.brainyquote.com/quotes/quotes/r/
      robertatki474958.html#lXDJumHzYHE5ZeIU.99.

thrive when it's fed with junk food. I have changed my eating habits and that binge on junk food cost me dearly!

MANAGING YOUR SPIRITUAL DIET

Robert Atkins was a cardiologist and creator of the famous Atkins Diet. In 2002, *Time* magazine named him one of the ten most influential people in America. His approach to dieting grew from his personal battle with obesity. In 1963, he weighed 224 pounds. He followed the advice and research of Dr. Alfred Pennington, who suggested removing all starch and sugar from meals. The plan worked, and the Atkins Diet was born.

Atkins knew junk food was dangerous to physical health, so he created an eating plan that, though controversial, produced positive results. He recognized that not all calories are the same.[18]

We should take Atkins' advice, and apply it to our spiritual lives: all religious activity is not the same. If we consume religious junk, we will become spiritually unhealthy. We see that lived out before us almost every day. People substitute spiritual "snacks" for nutritious meals, and the results aren't good.

We have created "junk food faith" by snacking instead of feasting on nutritional content. People often look for the quickest fix to satisfy their spiritual hunger pangs. And what does that look like in a practical sense? Junk food faith is biblical small talk rather than personal Bible study. It's substituting fellowship for stewardship. It's what happens when people take a "What's in it for me?" attitude to church.

In Psalm 92:4, the psalmist said, "You thrill me LORD, with all you have done for me! I sing for joy because of what you have done" (NLT).

---

18   Wikipedia, "Robert Atkins (nutritionist)," posted at http://en.wikipedia.org/
        wiki/Robert_Atkins_%28nutritionist%29.

That's what you were made for. You weren't made to participate in empty activity. The "empty activity" thrill sequence will leave you burned out. It will rob you of the vitality God intended for your life. Junk food faith makes you spiritually unhealthy and unenergetic.

> The world's thrill sequence will take the wind out of your spiritual sails because you'll be looking for thrills outside of God's plan for your life.

The world's thrill sequence will take the wind out of your spiritual sails because you'll be looking for thrills outside of God's plan for your life. It will be easy to rationalize what you're doing and, for a moment, it might be thrilling. Eventually, the thrill will vanish, and that experience won't provide the rush of adrenaline it provided the first time around. It will take more.

You will compromise in one or more areas of life. You will feel guilty at first. Remember Adam and Eve? After they sinned, they tried to hide from God. You will do the same thing. Rather than develop a stronger relationship with Him, it will get weaker. Before you know it, you will have a junk food faith.

You were made for more than that. You were made to say, "You thrill me, Lord, with all you've done for me! You thrill me!" That's not a boring faith. That's a healthy acknowledgment of God's goodness and mercy. Think about all God has done for you. If you can do that without a sense of awe and amazement, you are missing something.

NOT A FAST-FOOD GOD

Jesus has some words for people caught up in the thrill sequence. In Matthew 11:28-30, He says:

Come to me, all you who are weary and burdened, and I will
give you rest. Take my yoke upon you and learn from me,
for I am gentle and humble in heart, and you will find rest
for your souls. For my yoke is easy and my burden is light.

Jesus knows you are going to wear yourself out. Because He's
God, He knows when you are getting close to burnout. He knows
what's happening before your body ever realizes something's wrong.
Through His Word and the presence of the Holy Spirit, He comes to
you and says, "I know you are worn out. If you will come to me, I will
give you life. I will give you what you have really been looking for." He
knows what you are looking for even if you don't!

The *Westminster Catechism* says the chief end of man is to
glorify God and enjoy Him forever. That's it; you were made to enjoy
God. That's the thrill sequence He has for you. That's what will bring
you meaning—enjoying God and being in relationship with Him.
How long has it been since you have enjoyed being in a relationship
with God? Have you ever enjoyed a relationship with God? It's what
you were made for.

Only 25 percent of the population is living for something more
than themselves. That means only one-quarter of the people around
you are truly living for God. Sure, there are plenty of people who are
fans of God and sometimes participate in a religious activity, but
only one-quarter really live for God. That number, honestly, might
even be optimistic.

Those who live for God find their personal significance. They
see their lives the way God sees them—as valuable resources to be
invested for God's glory. For people with that mindset, it's a privilege
to serve Him. They can think of nothing they'd rather do. This is the
life God wants for you and me. This quality of existence isn't reserved
for the spiritually elite; it's available to everyone.

There's a difference in being thrilled *by* God and being thrilled *in* God. We are thrilled by a lot of things—our favorite team's last-second victory, a mouthwatering dessert, an unexpected refund, vacation days we didn't know we had, closing a huge deal, and no traffic on the morning commute. Those things thrill us.

What does it mean to be thrilled *in* God? It means we live within the context of our relationship with Him. He isn't one of the things that entertains us; He is the source of all that is good and meaningful. He is the focus of our lives. He is the real thrill.

Have you ever treated God like the mystery person behind the speaker box at a fast-food drive-thru? You know what I mean. You wait impatiently in a line of people who, like you, have decided not to get out of their cars and get a little exercise on their way to a mega meal. You get to the speaker box and place your order, hoping the person on the other end gets the details correct. Then, it's back to the impatient waiting while you creep toward the window where you pay for your order. Finally, you make it to the

> Those who live for God find their personal significance.

pickup window, where you receive at least a portion of the order you placed. Experience has taught you to verify the order before leaving the parking lot, so you pull over to the side only to discover that you didn't get everything you ordered. You put the car in park and head inside only to discover that there's no line. People who took the time to inconvenience themselves and get out of their cars are enjoying their meals while you explain to another person what went wrong with your order. Have you been there?

It's easy to grow frustrated when God doesn't deliver what you want according to your schedule. You are in a hurry, and He obviously isn't watching the clock. Suddenly, your faith has become more focused on what you want to receive than on who you are becoming and what you are doing for God. That's junk food faith. You are driven by God's willingness to deliver thrill after thrill toward your bucket list of faith. When the thrills stop, you find something else to do with your time.

THE GOD OF REAL THRILLS

When you are thrilled *in* God, your awareness of Him is more than situational. God is more than a hobby. You treat Him less like the drive-thru at your favorite burger or chicken joint and more like the loving Father He is.

You were made to break out of that thrill sequence and really live for God. When you do, you'll experience a whole new thrill sequence. Let me explain what I mean. Activities available to you as a follower of Jesus Christ lead to true happiness, joy, and satisfaction. This is the divine thrill sequence. To the casual observer, it doesn't look thrilling, but casual observers base their observations on faulty assumptions.

You see, casual observers believe real thrills can't possibly be found within a vibrant relationship with God. They view Him as the cosmic killjoy and the ultimate purveyor of boredom and irrelevance. Nothing is further from the truth. God created enjoyment because He created life. People who trust God know that is true.

A willful trust in God as your Maker brings you into the thrill sequence because you start living for more than this world. When disappointments come your way—and they will—you don't have to worry because you can say, "I trust Him."

When you trust Him, you live at a higher level than people chasing after other things. There is real joy available to you when you engage in heartfelt worship. You experience authentic peace when your life echoes your commitment to and relationship with

God. Suddenly, you spend your days differently. You discover what happiness really is, and you develop a new attitude toward life.

When you truly know God, you will want to know Him more. You will become passionate about pursuing the knowledge of God. You might ask, "Will a Bible study lead me into an authentic thrill sequence?" Absolutely! When a Scripture passage comes alive, you will learn more about God. It won't be boring; it will be emotional. It might bring tears to your eyes when you think about how much God loves you. You will be overwhelmed by His awesomeness and mercy. You will understand things you might have overlooked in the past. This causes a rush of excitement and joy.

> A willful trust in God as your Maker brings you into the thrill sequence because you start living for more than this world.

God's presence will overpower your self-doubt, and you will agree with God when He says, "You are whole. You are well."

When you live God's thrill sequence, you discover joy in some unusual places. You look for ways to be a more responsible steward of the resources God entrusts to you. You see opportunities to serve Him long before someone asks you to serve. You look for ways to use your talents for His glory because we all will have to stand in front of Him one day and give an account of what we did with our lives. When this happens, life becomes even more thrilling, and you have something to look forward to.

It will be a thrill sequence to talk about how much you can give to God and to others. How little do you need to live on? Can you live on less, so you can give more and more? This is a thrill sequence the world doesn't comprehend, an "empty-yourself" kind of thrill sequence. People you know are spending their lives on things that don't matter while you invest your life in things that will outlive you. Who is experiencing the real thrill sequence?

When you live God's thrill sequence, you sleep soundly because stress doesn't get the best of you. Few people know the kind of happiness that comes with God's thrill sequence because lesser things like sex, materialism, and gluttony are celebrated in our society, so people strive after those. What they don't realize is that they are stopping short of the best thing. It's like having the capacity to make an "A" but settling for a "C" because that's what everyone else is making.

If everyone else is doing it, it probably isn't a good idea. There's a difference between popularity and wisdom, and that's why the Bible has so much to say about wisdom. Take a look at Proverbs 13:20, "Become wise by walking with the wise; hang out with fools and watch your life fall to pieces" (*The Message*). The New International Version says, "Walk with the wise and become wise, for a companion of fools suffers harm." Look closely at that verse. It doesn't say you will become a fool by hanging out with fools; it says you will suffer harm, or your life will fall to pieces. Who wants that?

> The world's thrill sequence can make you temporarily happy, but that happiness evaporates quickly.

The world's thrill sequence offers no hope. It leads only to a dead end. You can run from thrill to thrill if you want, but in the end, you'll realize the foolishness of it all. The effort you put into achieving things to make yourself happy would be better spent focusing on your relationship with God. When we try to cram God into the cracks and crevices of our lives, we demonstrate our propensity to be fools.

Who are the fools? They are the ones settling for the world's thrill sequence. They are the ones who show contempt for God by pursuing self-gratification and a disregard for biblical guidelines. They are the ones who live for the next pleasure, take pictures, and celebrate themselves on social media. They are the ones who become famous on YouTube while remaining unfazed by God's amazing love.

The world's thrill sequence can make you temporarily happy, but that happiness evaporates quickly. Living for yourself won't make you happy, and you'll never discover life's meaning that way. There is a tension between wisdom and foolishness. Wisdom is God's way of looking at things; foolishness is the world's way. Sometimes, there is more encouragement to embrace foolishness than to pursue wisdom.

Think about it. The world says you should be a player in life. Society tells you marriage isn't necessary, commitment isn't cool, and that playing the field is far more enjoyable. God condemns sexual sin, encourages marital faithfulness, and expects all people to show the utmost respect for others. People who are players appear happy, but they are empty inside. The relationships and activities they think will bring them satisfaction aren't measuring up to their expectations. They paint on a smile and try to cover their misery, but it's there, and God knows what's going on.

Do you know what real joy is? Real joy is waking up every day next to the person you made a vow to and who will be with you for the rest of your lives. That's real joy. That's the thrill sequence. Do you know what real joy is? It's tucking your kids into bed every night and not having to visit them on Thursdays, and every other weekend.

The real thrill sequence is what your kids say to you at evening prayers and in the morning at breakfast. It's thrilling to do life with them. That's the thrill sequence. Real joy is found in investing your life rather than milking it for every ounce of self-gratification, because you don't find true joy living for yourself. It's junk food.

Proverbs 24:1–7 says:

Do not envy the wicked, do not desire their company; for their hearts plot violence, and their lips talk about making trouble. By wisdom a house is built, and through understanding it is established; through knowledge its rooms are filled with rare and beautiful treasures. The wise prevail through great power, and those who have knowledge muster their strength. Surely you need guidance to wage war, and victory is won through many advisers. Wisdom is too high for fools; in the assembly at the gate they must not open their mouths.

Life is a spiritual struggle. It's a tug of war between foolishness and wisdom—and you are the rope. Wisdom, powered by your relationship with God, pulls you toward right living and the real thrill sequence. Foolishness, powered by the philosophy of the world, pulls you toward temporary satisfaction. The power that wins is the power you feed the most.

You feed wisdom by studying God's Word, participating in group Bible studies, prayer, worship, and quiet contemplation of God's desires for your life. You feed foolishness by ignoring God's Word, making your relationship with Him little more than a hobby, and devoting your discretionary resources—time, talent, money, influence—to things that have little or no eternal significance.

When wisdom builds your house, it's amazing! We were made to enjoy God; that is the ultimate thrill sequence. We were made to be thrilled by the Lord. We were made to swim in an ocean of pleasure and leave the mud puddles of the world's thrill sequence. God said He created you for so much more than a boring, unsatisfying life. He has more for you than a "chase everything that doesn't matter" life. The good news is that whoever you are and wherever you are, you don't have to be stuck in the wrong thrill sequence.

Let's go back and look at a passage we mentioned earlier in this chapter, Matthew 11:28–30. Jesus invites you to come to Him. If you're weary, worn down, and broken, come to Jesus, and He will give you rest. He will give you what you're looking for. He will fill the hole in your life and give you real meaning.

That's what the psalmist said, too: "You show me the path of life. In your presence there is fullness of joy; in your right hand are pleasures forevermore" (Psalm 16:11, NRSV). That's it. That's the thrill sequence. You were made to pursue God and to break out of the world's thrill sequence. You were created to find meaning in Jesus Christ. His invitation is open to everyone, and the real question is: will you accept it?

KEY IDEAS

- If we consume religious junk, we will become spiritually unhealthy.

- The world's thrill sequence will take the wind out of your spiritual sails because you will be looking for thrills outside of God's plan for your life.

- Only 25 percent of the population is living for something more than themselves.

- If everyone else is doing it, it probably isn't a good idea.

- Life is a spiritual struggle. The power that wins is the power you feed the most.

DISCUSSION QUESTIONS

1. What does your spiritual vibrancy reveal about your spiritual diet? What nutritional adjustments do you need to make to become spiritually healthy?

2. Make a list of some of the things that thrill you. Place a "W" by the ones that are most consistent with the world's philosophy and a "G" by the ones that are consistent with God's point of view. How authentic is your thrill sequence?

3. Look back over the past week. What has influenced your activity more: the world's opportunities or your commitment to God? Explain your response.

4. Which power—worldly or spiritual—do you feed the most? Based on your response, which power is winning the battle for control of your life?

ACTION STEPS

1. Use your journal to record your thoughts as you commit yourself to being more intentional about spending time with God.

2. As you participate in religious activities, evaluate the outcomes to see if what you are consuming is spiritually nutritious or junk food.

chapter five

GOD'S COMPETITION

"I am disturbed when I see the majority of so-called Christians having such little understanding of the real nature of the faith they profess. Faith is a subject of such importance that we should not ignore it because of the distractions or the hectic pace of our lives."[19]

—WILLIAM WILBERFORCE

AS I POINTED OUT in chapter 1, "busy" is the new "fine." Ask someone how he's doing, and he might say, "I've been real busy." Ask a mom how her week was, and she will probably say in exasperation, "Busy!" "What does next week look like for you?" "Busy." "How was the Christmas break?" "We were super busy!" I know you have heard these kinds of responses, and I'm confident most people have declared their busyness within the past few days. Although we complain about being busy, we think that's how we are supposed to be. We think we

---

19   BrainyQuote, posted at http://www.brainyquote.com/quotes/quotes/w/williamwil618055.html#doPTotmGd732Hdcz.99.

need to be stimulated and entertained. The busier people are, the more accomplished they feel. Remember experience cramming? But what are they busy doing, and why is all of this activity necessary?

THE BIG TO-DO ABOUT GOD

I believe many are chasing the thrill sequence to find what they lost. They try to rev it up or dull it down, but the things of this world never fill them up. Our restlessness is people looking for what we have lost. We try and chase the thrill and simultaneously dull our pain.

People find the time to do what they think is important or valuable. They budget time the same way they budget money, except there's no time "credit card" available when they run short. You start each day with twenty-four hours. You allocate some to sleeping, personal care, eating, working, school, taking care of kids, and so forth. Once you allocate time for all the things you have to do, you choose which items get your discretionary time. That's where hobbies, social activities, shopping, exercise, and the like come in.

So, where does your relationship with God fit in these categories? Is it in the "must do" list or the "if there's time" list? In today's culture, many people put it on the second list, and some put it extremely low on the second list.

What happens when you run out of time before you run out of things to do? You turn the page, reset the calendar, and start over. Things left undone yesterday probably won't make the cut today. How did we get to the point where our relationships with God garner little more than hobby status? Why are we more interested in pleasure than in spiritual development? It might be that the church hasn't presented a compelling alternative.

I don't think the church should have to compete with society. I believe a dynamic relationship with God is attractive by itself. I do think, however, that we have allowed the exercise of religion to become more important than a life of faith. Too many people today have great relationships with their churches but spend little or no time with God.

> Too many people today have great relationships with their churches but spend little or no time with God.

What happens when we worship *worship?* The hour spent gathered together becomes the total expression of our faith relationship with God. It can become an emotional high we expect to surpass the following week, but that's not a sustainable model.

Other things compete with our relationships with God as well. It's impossible to list everything that distracts us or contends with our spiritual commitment. It's best to simply take a few moments and think how we make decisions about the things we do and don't do.

There are two forces that contribute to our perpetual state of distraction. First, we have instant access to more information than our minds can process. Second, the inventions people thought would make us more efficient have, in fact, become major distractions. I'm talking about technology. Our minds are not equipped to deal with everything coming at us, and we don't have a good system for making decisions.

One study revealed that office workers waste 2.1 hours per day on distractions. A separate study discovered that people average eleven minutes on a task before giving in to a distraction and then spend twenty-five minutes getting back to the place they were before the distraction.[20] I bet if you are reading this on an electronic device or with a phone nearby, it's a struggle for you to stay focused on this

---

20   David Rock, "Easily Distracted: Why It's Hard to Focus, and What to Do about It," *Psychology Today,* posted at http://www.psychologytoday.com/blog/your-brain-work/200910/easily-distracted-why-its-hard-focus-and-what-do-about-it.

book. While I was writing it, I had to put all my devices on airplane mode just to stay focused!

The same things that distract us from our work distract us from our intentional spiritual development. You have probably sat down with the intention of reading or studying your Bible, only to be distracted by something happening around you. (Stick with me—don't get distracted—because this is important.)

When you aren't growing spiritually, your relationship with God becomes stale. Good or bad, your relationship with God is contagious. It affects everyone around you. As a result, many churches lack attractive vibrancy because people lack individual vibrancy in their lives. People see what our faith does for us and choose to do something else with their time.

How did our faith become so boring? Why are people more attracted to outside activities than spiritual matters? It might be because we have inadvertently relegated spirituality to church attendance. In other words, God is real only when you are at church. Therefore, if church is boring, God must be boring.

> Good or bad, your relationship with God is contagious. It affects everyone around you.

Although that's the way many people feel, it's not true. God is the most amazing, loving, exciting force anywhere. Our boredom with Him doesn't accurately reflect His awesomeness. The church often fails to present God the way He really is. That's why some people would rather go shopping or to a ballgame than to church. At least the merchandise on the shelves at the store is occasionally new, and the game could have an unexpected outcome.

That might sound cynical, but keep in mind that I am a pastor. I understand the responsibility the church has for presenting Christ to a doubting world, and I know it's my responsibility as a pastor to lead that effort. It's a big job because the world is becoming less and less receptive to our faith.

Think about it this way. The average person "out there" has the option of going to a football game where eighty thousand people cheer relentlessly for a team that might not be very good. The same person could choose your church. If that person is looking for excitement and companionship with excited people, which option will they choose? A few churches have a feel of authentic excitement. Others struggle simply to put on a good show and, sadly, others don't even try. The church has to do better!

Lights and fog machines are not the issue; authenticity is. Rock music or hymns sung by a choir don't matter if there is no spirit of vibrancy within the congregation. I tell people all the time, "Who cares what type of music you sing as long as it moves you!" Our enthusiasm for God isn't external to us; it's internal. The problem isn't what the church is doing; it's who the people in the church believe God is.

> The problem isn't what the church is doing; it's who the people in the church believe God is.

This isn't a new phenomenon. Read Luke 11:37–54. Much like the first century, our culture is full of rules. We have traffic rules, travel rules, rules at work, and rules about when to file our taxes. Rules generally are intended to correct or control an undesired behavior. When things get out of control, new rules are established.

CHECK-LIST FAITH

In Jesus' day, religion was characterized by rules—more than seven hundred rules governed Jewish life. It was a full-time job to monitor adherence to the rules, and that responsibility fell to a group of leaders called Pharisees. They became Jesus' most aggressive opponents.

Because Jesus challenged the status quo, it seems odd that a Pharisee would invite Jesus into his home. As with most interactions between Jesus and the Pharisees, the religious leader had an ulterior motive. This Pharisee wanted to challenge Jesus in a social setting, so he could discredit the Lord publicly.

Promoting adherence to religious rules isn't the best marketing strategy. It didn't work in the first century, and it won't work today. But it's hard to keep rules out of our religion even though many of the rules have no biblical basis at all. In spite of the fact that rules-based religion is objectionable, faith is still presented as a heavy burden to bear. The world doesn't respond favorably to rule-loving religious zealots. Unbelievers see rules as hindrances to an authentic relationship with Jesus. People looking for excuses to resist a relationship with Christ don't have to look very hard.

Not all rules are bad. Many are intended to provide order, and order is a characteristic of God. Too many rules, however, make our faith heavy and unbearable. When being a Christ-follower appears to be more restrictive than it is freeing, most people will not be interested.

Take another look at Luke 11:37–54. The Pharisees were always concerned about their religious *appearance*. There were rules to govern almost everything they did, including washing before a meal. It's interesting that they were concerned about their reputations but unconcerned about their relationships with God.

The Bible says the host was surprised when Jesus didn't participate in a ceremonial washing before His meal. This was expected of all obedient Jews. The rules, however, had no biblical basis. In choosing not to wash before eating, Jesus wasn't showing disrespect toward God; He was setting up a teaching opportunity.

Jesus, of course, knew what the man was thinking. His thought process was consistent with what many people think today: righteousness is a matter of what a person does. In other words, people then and now think their thoughts and attitudes have no bearing on their relationship with Christ. They are safe as long as they do the right things. This is a hypocritical approach to faith that is unappealing to others.

> Reputation is what others think of you, but character is what God thinks of you.

Jesus' words cut to the heart of the matter. Our external behaviors and internal thoughts cannot be separated. Whenever we attempt to act in a way that is inconsistent with our attitudes or beliefs, we become like the Pharisees. While eating, Jesus probably pointed to a cup on the table. He said that the inside and outside of the cup were connected. It would be ridiculous to clean the outside of the cup and leave the inside dirty. Likewise, it's ridiculous for us to act like believers but refuse to let God's truth renew our minds.

The Pharisees based their behaviors on the interpretation of the Law provided by the scribes. So when Jesus began addressing problematic issues, He spoke first about the Pharisees and then about the foundational interpretations of the scribes. Every outward behavior has a core belief. Jesus dealt with both.

The "woes" Jesus expressed in this passage are similar to those found in Matthew 23. Jesus began by calling attention to the Pharisees and their hypocrisy. The Pharisees were extremely careful about tithing everything, even the mint leaves they owned. Jesus pointed out that tithing is good, but the Pharisees had ignored their responsibility to demonstrate mercy and forgiveness. Jesus wasn't telling them to stop tithing; He simply said that tithing doesn't buy

God's favor. Tithing without having a right relationship with God is little more than donating to a charitable organization.

The Pharisees were also more concerned about their reputations than their character. Reputation is what *others* think of you, but character is what *God* thinks of you. The Pharisees thought keeping the rules was all they needed to do. They forgot that God looks on the hearts of men and women.

The Jews had specific guidelines for handling dead bodies. They even had to be careful about walking over graves. Jesus' words, therefore, certainly incited their anger. He said the Pharisees were like dead men. Therefore, anyone who encountered them was defiled. Rather than helping people in their relationships with God, the Pharisees were actually harming people. If we don't watch it, we will hinder others from finding real faith and the only thing that will satisfy them.

Though the scribes were smart guys, the comment by one of them shows a lapse in judgment. He said, "Jesus, when you criticize the Pharisees, you are insulting us, as well." Jesus used this teachable moment to challenge their understanding about faith in God. Jesus said that the scribes loaded people down with a heavy burden. He was talking about the rules Jews were required to follow. They were oppressive and unreasonable. The scribes also were guilty of celebrating the prophets without acknowledging the role their ancestors played in their deaths. Finally, the scribes made God's Word inaccessible to common people. The scribes made people believe that understanding God's Word was impossible. This was job security for the scribes, because when the people were neither challenged nor motivated to dig into God's Word they waited for someone to tell them what it said.

There is an eerie parallel between what Jesus encountered and the state of religion today. Some people still act like Pharisees. They believe they own God and that people can experience Him only if they hear it from them. Hypocrites get angry when their sin is revealed. Remember, hypocrites are more concerned about their reputations than their character.

The Enemy wants us to be hypocrites because he knows our testimonies will be discredited. He wants us to focus on the rules, look for ways to get around them, and then encourage others to do the same. He wants us to make our relationships with God all about us. He wants us to be so busy that we settle for a version of faith that is nothing like the faith we see in the pages of Scripture.

It's easy to reduce the Bible to a set of rules and regulations. As believers, we must discover the universal principles that underlie each rule. We must be aware that our freedom should never allow us to become a stumbling block to others. If what we do might cause someone to question God's existence, we are obligated to stop.

When we focus on rules, we become legalistic. When we focus on relationship with God, we won't need rules to govern our behavior. Authentic, growing Christ-followers don't need rules. That kind of faith is attractive and powerful!

KEY IDEAS

- "Busy" is the new "fine."

- The church shouldn't have to compete with society; a dynamic relationship with God is attractive by itself.

- The same things that distract us from our work distract us from our intentional spiritual development.

- Our enthusiasm for God isn't external to us; it is internal. The problem isn't what the church is doing; it's who the people in the church believe God is.

- Our freedom should never allow us to become a stumbling block to others.

DISCUSSION QUESTIONS

1. What are some things that keep you busy? How would you describe the spiritual effect of those things on your life? Are they positive or negative factors? Explain your response.

2. If someone was curious about the importance of a relationship with God and your life was the determining factor, would that person choose to follow God or not? Why?

3. What are some of the things that easily distract you from growing in your relationship with God? Why do you let those things distract you?

4. Who do you believe God is, and to what degree does your lifestyle support your statement?

ACTION STEPS

1. Use your journal to keep track of how you spend time each day. Look for things that keep you busy or distract you. Then plan a strategy for getting around those things.

2. View your life as the only evidence someone might have for what it means to be a believer. Look for ways to make your relationship with God more authentic and contagious.

chapter six

NOT ENOUGH

"Many churches of all persuasions are hiring research agencies to poll neighborhoods, asking what kind of church they prefer. Then the local churches design themselves to fit the desires of the people. True faith in God that demands selflessness is being replaced by trendy religion that serves the selfish."[21]

—BILLY GRAHAM

WHAT DID GOD HAVE in mind when He created the church? When you scan the landscape of Christianity today, you see a variety of disconnected answers to that question. Each institution believes it has the correct answer for its context. Somehow, we have reduced church to something people attend when it's convenient. Many churches even plan for low attendance or societal distractions, but I don't think that's what God had in mind.

---

21   BrainyQuote, posted at http://www.brainyquote.com/quotes/quotes/b/
billygraha626304.html#4VIcKTjeUR2R7loe.99.

BACK TO THE FAITH

The New Testament church wasn't anything like our churches today. It didn't have a building, full-time pastor, team of paid musicians, parking lot, or video-based curriculum. The early church didn't even have the Bible as we know it today because much of the New Testament hadn't been written. Don't get me wrong; these things aren't bad in and of themselves. They just weren't necessary for the church to thrive in its early days.

The best way to describe the early church is with the word *family*. Though many people had extended family nearby, the Bible suggests that the spiritual bond was as strong as and, sometimes, more meaningful than the family connection.

The images that come to mind when you think about your family will affect the way you view anything presented by that analogy. A strong, dynamic family might make you think about the church in a positive light. However, a dysfunctional family might make you wonder about the appropriateness of the analogy. My family was so strong it's hard for me to think of it any other way. But through all of my counseling, I've discovered that the term *family* can bring up a lot of bad baggage.

Family is an accurate image of what it means to be in God's church.

Nonetheless, the Bible presents the church as the family of faith. Jesus called us "sons and daughters" of God. That makes all of us brothers and sisters. I'm glad, however, that we don't have to use that title with each other! I was in a church once where the people called me "Brother Rob," and it felt a little awkward. I'm sure they meant it as family, but it felt too formal to be family. It is true, however, that God is our Father, and as His children, we have an inheritance. Therefore, *family* is an accurate image of what it means to be in God's church.

Pastor and author Chuck Swindoll said, "A family is a place where principles are hammered and honed on the anvil of everyday living."[22] That is true about our earthly families. It's also true about the family of faith. This "hammering and honing" is why God gave us the church.

When we reduce our idea of church to a place where we gather, sing, and study God's Word, we've missed the point. Church isn't a place for us to gather and watch performances. It isn't an activity in which we participate because it wards off some pending doom. It's not a good-luck charm, fortune cookie, or lottery ticket. It's God's family.

Acts 4:13 says Peter was "unschooled and ordinary." We remember him for his impulsive behavior and blatant denial of Christ. His companions knew him as a fisherman. Jesus saw him as an accurate example of humanity.

Jesus asked Peter, "Who do you say that I am?" And Peter answered, "You are the Messiah, the Son of the living God" (Matthew 16:16). At times, Peter understood things few others grasped. At other times, he demonstrated his lack of knowledge and wavering faith. It stands to reason, therefore, that God would use this man who so accurately reflects our lives to encourage the early church—and the church today. We can all relate to Peter. We can all relate to his message.

Peter understood that faith in Jesus Christ should affect the way people live. Yet he also understood that faith in Jesus Christ gives us insight into our best possible lives. We should be encouraged by Peter's example and his words. We should be challenged by the power of his words in our lives.

---

22   BrainyQuote, posted at http://www.brainyquote.com/quotes/quotes/c/charlesrs155778.html.

Peter grasped the idea of God's family as a community of faith. He was one of Jesus' disciples and knew how important the other disciples were to his spiritual development. Not everyone, however, got it. By the time Peter wrote his letters to the church, there was some confusion about what it meant to be a part of God's family.

The Christian community was in its infancy, and those who were a part of it had different expectations about God and the faith community. Some believers grew up in the Jewish faith. Others came from pagan families. However, once they accepted Jesus Christ as their Savior, they became part of one family.

The differences between individuals eventually showed. There were interpersonal conflicts and public arguments that affected the faith community negatively. People didn't always get along.

Some things never change, right? In 1 Peter 1:22–2:12, Peter addressed the issue of Christian unity and encouraged believers to view church as an opportunity to celebrate their common faith foundation and to allow the church to be the launching pad for a movement with the power to change the world. That's a radical departure from the idea that church is all about kids' VBS activities, choirs, musicals, and laser lights.

RELATIONSHIPS NOW AND LATER

If we are going to escape our human version of the thrill sequence, we must redefine what it means to be part of God's church. It's not a place we go; it's the environment where we do everything that matters. It's our family, not a function on the calendar.

We build relationships based on our perceived commonalities. We gather with people who have something in common with us. Think about it. What do you have in common with the people living in your neighborhood? What do you have in common with the people who sit beside you in church? What are some of the differences between you and your neighbors or you and fellow believers? Is it easier to identify your similarities or differences?

It often seems easier to identify our differences. Differences form the boundaries that separate us from each other, and when we focus on the

> If we are going to escape our human version of the thrill sequence, we must redefine what it means to be part of God's church.

differences, we find it hard to partner with others. Growing together doesn't happen. This is dangerous in society and debilitating in the faith community.

Satan knows that Christian relationships are a powerful force—which is why he works so hard to destroy them. You can be very lonely in the midst of a crowded room. You may think you are doing something beneficial, but you are being lulled to sleep and are, in fact, lethargic. As believers, we are responsible for guarding our faith family and growing closer to God, together.

Peter understood some basic truths about the church and reminded his readers that they all entered the community through the same door. They shared a common past: they were sinners separated from God. Some people still believe, however, that they are believers because they were born into a Christian home, attended a Christian school, or participate regularly in religious activities. But those aren't doors that lead to becoming part of the family of faith.

Only our faith relationship with Christ ensures our future in heaven and God's presence in our daily lives. We sometimes forget the latter. As believers, we are all beneficiaries of God's unmerited favor. There is nothing we can do to earn God's forgiveness. He paid our debt by giving His Son as a sacrifice for our sins. For that, we should be eternally grateful.

It's the attitude of gratefulness that unifies all believers. It's also the foundation upon which the church is established. As believers, we have a lot in common:

- We have the same Holy Spirit living inside each of us (1 Corinthians 12:13)
- We have access to the same Father (1 Peter 1:17)
- We trust the same Word of God (1 Peter 1:23)

It is important to grasp what Peter said to his readers. He warned them against interpersonal attitudes that have the potential of disrupting our unity within the family of faith—malice, deceit, hypocrisy, envy, and slander. All of these things have the potential to harm our relationships with others. So how do we prevent these attitudes? Peter offered a solution. He told his readers (and us) to grow up spiritually. That happens within the family of faith.

Spiritual growth will choke out a lot of immature behaviors and attitudes. Your relationship with God should be your top priority. The church isn't here to make you grow; it's here to equip you to serve God. Your spiritual growth is your personal responsibility. It's part of being in the family!

READY TO BE REMARKABLE

Why is it important to grow up in your relationship with God? What does God want to equip you for? Peter didn't leave his readers wondering what to do. He wanted them to experience a thrill sequence unlike any they had ever experienced, and the same is available to us today!

We see the pattern of the religious thrill sequence in the lives of the Israelites. We know how often they let God down. Their spiritual inconsistencies are well-documented in the Bible, in the Old Testament. We don't need to imitate them; we should learn from them.

The Israelites lost sight of their purpose. The more self-centered they became, the further they drifted from God. Their drift usually led to calamity, which forced them to return to God—for a season. Then, as life settled down, they resumed their self-centered living. They drifted, suffered the consequences, and returned to God. We see that cycle over and over. This was their thrill sequence.

Even though we know what happened when the Israelites disappointed God, we still follow their example. We let our relationship with God become all about us and what we get. Our self-centeredness causes us to drift away from God. Life happens, a crisis erupts, and we turn back toward God.

Peter reminded his readers that God chose them for something more than perpetual futility. He chose them to live extraordinary lives. We were chosen for the same purpose. We are here to know God and to make Him known.

So why is that so hard? Why do we still lack vitality in our spiritual lives? Like the Israelites, we easily lose sight of our purpose. We aren't here to blend into the scenery. God left us here to change our communities, our culture, and the world. We are here to remind people of their need for Jesus.

> God left us here to change our communities, our culture, and the world. We are here to remind people of their need for Jesus.

Peter reminded his readers that the world rejected Jesus, and we should, therefore, expect rejection. The apostle James knew the problems associated with trying to be like the world while claiming to be a believer. James 4:4 says, "You adulterous people, don't you know that friendship with the world means enmity against God? Therefore, anyone who chooses to be a friend of the world becomes an enemy of God."

You can be like the world and abandon your purpose, or you can give God's thrill sequence a try. Your decision will determine your spiritual vitality. Like Jesus, you might be rejected by people who prefer their thrill sequence. You might lose some friends. You might reconsider some of your social activities. Everything you do reveals to the world what you really think about Jesus.

It's not easy to step off of the world's rollercoaster. It's easy to think God has no use for you. After all, you know your past. That's why it's hard to accept Peter's declaration that you are part of a community of "chosen people, a royal priesthood, a holy nation, God's special possession" (1 Peter 2:9). You know your sins. You know your weaknesses. You know you are unworthy of God's love.

And you are right. You aren't worthy of anything good God offers. Yet, because He loves you, He offers it anyway. You have access to unconditional forgiveness. You can live in the reality of underserved mercy.

That's a threat to Satan's schemes. He wants you to believe you can have a meaningful life apart from a relationship with God. He wants you to give in to the world's pressures. He also wants you to fail God. That's why Peter included a stern warning in 1 Peter 2:11: "Dear friends, I urge you, as foreigners and exiles, to abstain from sinful desires, which wage war against your soul."

As believers, we should "abstain from sinful desires"—anything that contradicts God's character. Sinful desires are those attitudes and actions that disappoint God. The things-that-disappoint-God list is a pretty long one! You will never honor God by focusing on things you shouldn't do. You need to focus on things you should do. Peter continued his admonition in the next verse: "Live such good lives among the pagans that, though they accuse you of doing wrong, they may see your good deeds and glorify God on the day he visits us" (1 Peter 2:12).

Focus on honoring God with your life. That's how God will use you to change your community and the world. Peter knew the futility of empty religion. He knew that many people came from backgrounds where they just went through religious motions, believing God would be impressed with their participation. He understood the struggles that the early believers faced because he faced them, too.

Peter encourages us to consider our lives from God's perspective. He pushes back against society's norms and challenges believers to adopt a higher standard—a higher standard that is needed today. Otherwise, the faith we claim has no power at all.

God created the church to be an agent of change in the world. The church is here to equip and empower you to live out your giftedness. It is here to motivate you to dig deeper into God's Word and to apply its principles to your life. The church is here to do much more than you may realize.

This is your family. These are the people you turn to when times are tough. These are the people with whom you celebrate God's goodness and the great things that happen in your life. Life is full of ups and downs, and you aren't going to understand some of the things that happen. Within the family of faith, though, you will find comfort and reassurance. One day, your experiences will encourage someone else. Your experiences will open the door for you to help others see God in the midst of situations they don't understand.

We can change our communities when we help people understand just how powerful God is. You and I know what He does in our lives. As He enables and strengthens us, we are able to go into our communities and help alleviate suffering, feed the hungry, train those who are seeking jobs, and deliver hope to those who have given up on life.

That's the ministry God has given to each of us. The church is here to help us do what God has called us to do. When we get involved showing God's love to others, we will discover church in a new light. This was God's plan from the beginning.

KEY IDEAS

- The New Testament church looked a lot different than our churches today.

- The Bible presents the church as the family of faith.

- If we are going to escape our version of the thrill sequence, we must redefine what it means to be a part of God's church. It's not a place we go; it's the environment where we do everything that matters.

- Spiritual growth will choke out a lot of immature behaviors and attitudes.

- God created the church to be an agent of change in the world. The church is here to equip and empower you to live out your giftedness.

DISCUSSION QUESTIONS

1. What words come to mind when you think about *church*? How does your description compare to the New Testament description of church?

2. Is your involvement in church more about what you get or how you invest your life? Explain your response.

3. How does your church experience compare to your understanding of *family*? What characteristics of family do you see in your church relationships?

4. Think about your spiritual life over the last six months. In what ways have you grown spiritually, and what things have helped you grow?

5. If you were a spiritual entrepreneur, what ministry would you start and why?

ACTION STEPS

1. Record in your journal some thoughts related to your idea of church, and then take some time to compare your thoughts to the biblical description of the church. Note what you learn about church from studying God's Word.

2. Write down some spiritual growth goals for the next three, six, and twelve months. Where do you want to be, spiritually, in each time frame? Track your progress by listing some measurable goals.

chapter seven

IS PLEASURE BAD?

"Man cannot live without joy; therefore when he is deprived of true spiritual joys it is necessary that he become addicted to carnal pleasures."[23]

—THOMAS AQUINAS

THE DICTIONARY DEFINES pleasure as "enjoyment or satisfaction derived from what is to one's liking."[24] So it makes sense that finding pleasure or satisfaction is a natural drive. Does anyone look forward to things they do *not* enjoy? Of course not!

Pleasure, however, can become addictive. Maybe you've seen a television show about people who hoard things. Some of the images are horrifying. Hoarding happens when people can't get enough of something. It's a psychological problem many of us don't understand.

---

23   BrainyQuote, posted at http://www.brainyquote.com/quotes/quotes/t/ thomasaqui186904.html.

24   Dictionary.com, "pleasure," posted at http://dictionary.reference.com/ browse/pleasure?s=t.

My wife thinks I'm a hoarder because I grab hotel pens whenever I'm at a good hotel. Not just one or two, I have been known to get one or two dozen if they are nice pens. (I feel so much better for sharing that, and maybe my recovery is now underway!)

You probably aren't a hoarder, but there may well be things you collect—figurines, porcelain roosters, or old coins perhaps. You might collect cars, houses, or DVDs. People have been collecting for a long time. Collecting reflects our pleasures.

SAVE IT AND CRAVE IT

The things we collect affect our allocation of resources. If we collect cars, we build garages. If we collect porcelain roosters, we build shelves. If we collect experiences, we create picture galleries or albums. Sometimes, we reminisce about the items we have collected and the pleasures we have experienced.

Some people might argue that pleasure is bad. God, however, created us with a desire for pleasure. He gave us a world that offers all kinds of pleasures, and the Bible says He "richly provides us everything for our enjoyment" (1 Timothy 6:17). So the question isn't whether pleasure is bad or good. The question is about what things bring us pleasure. Does our pleasure reflect adoration of God, or has our pleasure *replaced* God? Has the thrill sequence quenched the One who should thrill us?

When pleasure becomes our focus, coveting becomes our mode of operation. The dictionary defines *covet* as to "wish, long, or crave for something, especially the property of another person."[25] Wow! We do that a lot, don't we? We see what brings others pleasure, and we set our sights on doing what they did. Coveting is the root cause of many

---

25   The Free Dictionary website, "covet," posted at http://www.thefreedictionary. com/.

sins and vices. It was dangerous in biblical times, and it remains dangerous today.

We have all said, "If only I had . . ." followed by one or more things we believe would improve the quality of our lives. Sometimes it's a job, sometimes money, maybe a house; it could be an experience, or perhaps a car. It also can be

> Does our pleasure reflect adoration of God, or has our pleasure *replaced* God?

a relationship, social status, degree, or fame. Take a close look, and you will see the common thread—the one characteristic shared by everything we covet. They all focus on us. This is yet one more example of the thrill sequence.

Coveting is rooted in selfishness and self-gratification. James, the half-brother of Jesus, saw coveting as a hindrance to spiritual growth and vitality (James 4:1–3):

> What causes fights and quarrels among you? Don't they come from your desires that battle within you? You desire but do not have, so you kill. You covet but you cannot get what you want, so you quarrel and fight. You do not have because you do not ask God. When you ask, you do not receive, because you ask with wrong motives, that you may spend what you get on your pleasures.

It makes sense. We can either focus on getting what we want or on doing what God wants. The two attitudes are mutually exclusive. When the Israelites left Egypt, some non-Jews accompanied them. In Numbers 11:4, they are referred to as the "rabble" or riffraff. We don't know why they left Egypt. Maybe they feared the Egyptians more than they feared the uncertainty of leaving. Their presence among the Israelites is important, though, because they represent a group of people who created a huge distraction.

The non-Jews caused a great deal of trouble for the Israelites and Moses. These people were inside the camp, yet they didn't have a dynamic relationship with God. They were troublemakers and complainers. Along for the ride, they thought life was all about them.

You might know people like that. You might even be one of those people. When you don't get your way, you might complain. In fact, you *probably* complain. Have you ever had to "explain" a situation to someone to get an issue resolved? Complaining has been around for a long time because we are into self-gratification. We know what we want, and we don't like having to wait for it to arrive.

In Numbers 11:4–20, there is a fascinating story about a situation Israel faced because of the rabble. The non-Jews complained about the lack of food because food was their pleasure. The non-Jews thought the food was bland and predictable, and they were right. They ate manna all the time. Manna didn't bring them any pleasure because they remembered the food choices they had in Egypt. There they had meat, fish, cucumbers, melons, leeks, onions, garlic, and more. But since leaving Egypt, their diet had been reduced to manna—a white substance about the size of coriander seed. They tried to be creative with it, but there was only so much they could do. I'm sure it became monotonous to eat manna every day.

> People who live for pleasure always find themselves in captivity. It accompanies self-gratification.

Should their food have been such a big deal? No. People who live for pleasure have a way of focusing on life's insignificant details. Food is fuel. It provides the energy we need to live the life God intends. To the non-Jews and some of the Israelites, food became their source of pleasure. What they had in the past was more enjoyable than the current options, and they longed to satisfy their stomachs—even if it meant going back into captivity. I don't know how they cooked their leeks and cucumbers, but eating vegetables while being in slavery could not have been better than being a free people eating manna!

You might complain about the lack of sports networks on your cable service or the number of shoes in your closet. You might complain that your boss is unreasonable, the commute too long, or the parking inconvenient. People who like to complain will find something to complain about. But people who live for pleasure always find themselves in captivity. It accompanies self-gratification.

People today are captive to credit card companies because they thought a new wardrobe, furniture, or vacations would bring them pleasure. Others are in captivity to jobs they hate because the salary enables a self-indulgent lifestyle. Just like in the Bible, we trade freedom for captivity if it means getting what we want. That's the tragic thrill sequence many people live in today.

MANNA-FEST DESTINY

Long-term gain often requires short-term sacrifice. The Israelites were promised a land of their own—land offering fertile soil and culinary variety. Getting there, however, wouldn't be easy. If they would only focus on the journey more than themselves, they would see manna as God's provision. Yet what God provided and what they wanted were not the same. Their complaints revealed their true allegiance. They were fans of God, but were committed to living for pleasure. It sounds familiar, doesn't it?

What started as a complaint about the food by some outsiders spread throughout the camp. The Bible says people from every family complained outside Moses' tent. Their complaints were intense.

They wailed as if someone had died. Though they had everything they needed, they were distraught. Why? Because they didn't have everything they *wanted*. You've probably been there.

Every night when the dew fell, God provided manna. This was an incredible act of love. After all, the Israelites were traveling through the wilderness. There weren't many farms and fruit stands along the way. Rather than acknowledge God's provision, the Israelites complained.

How much like the Israelites are we? We have been blessed beyond measure. We have more than we need. We can make choices about what to eat, where to go, and how much to spend. We live in such a steady state of pleasure, that we often overlook God's gracious provisions.

The daily manna collection was an opportunity for the Israelites to celebrate God's goodness and to worship Him. But they turned worship into wailing by focusing on their wants. The same thing happens in our lives today. Like the Israelites, we often ignore what God has provided and complain about what we don't have. We have become religious consumers, not authentic Christ-followers. For too many, worship is something that happens in a big room at the church; it's not a way of life.

Had it not been for God, the Israelites wouldn't have had any manna to collect. Its presence was tangible evidence of God's presence, goodness, and love. Though we don't have manna, we do have tangible evidence of God's love today. But, much like the Israelites, we focus on ourselves and complain about the very things that should cause us to worship the One who provides for us.

The Israelites' behavior angered Moses. God was mad, too. He had delivered them from captivity, protected them from danger, provided everything they needed to survive, and delivered fresh manna every day. Yet they complained because they missed the fish and onions.

We fall into the same trap. God has saved us from an eternity in hell. He provides everything we need, protects us from danger (including ourselves), and guides us through His Word. In return, we complain because we don't have this or that. God would be completely justified in being mad at our complaints of what we're lacking. Our worship would be more meaningful if we focused on what God has done rather than on what we don't have.

Since the Israelites wouldn't stop complaining, God told Moses to gather seventy leaders in order to disperse the responsibility for managing the Israelites. He established a system that would allow Moses to stop dealing with complaints, so he could focus on

> Our worship would be more meaningful if we focused on what God has done rather than on what we don't have.

leadership. Then God gave Moses a message for the complainers: They would get meat, and lots of it. They would eat it every day for a month. They would have so much that they would get sick of it. God even said they would have so much meat it would come out of their nostrils! (Numbers 11:20) (Note to self: no complaining when God's providing!)

Living for the next pleasure can be debilitating. We get so focused on ourselves and what we want that we stop looking at why we are here and where we should be going. It's easy to believe God is holding out on us. We think we know what we need better than He does. This is how we spiritualize our thrill sequences.

Like children, we hyper-focus on something we desire. We see someone else with something we want. We can't stop thinking about it. We press the pause button on life, waiting for our desire to be fulfilled.

God gave the complainers what they wanted, and they quickly discovered it wasn't as great as they thought it would be. That's why we must be careful what we ask. If we keep on asking, we might discover a truth we really prefer not to know.

ALWAYS MORE TO WANT

Do you love pleasure more than you love God? If so, that's an idol. An idol is anything that would make you upset if it were taken from you. That's probably not what you were thinking an idol was, and hopefully that makes you stop and think. Many things fall into that category—jobs, people, possessions, appearance, sporting events. Nothing you have belongs to you; it's all on loan from God. What He allows others to have is His business. You should celebrate the manna!

Advertisers constantly remind us of all the things we don't have that we deserve. These things we so deserve are parked in the driveways of perfectly groomed homes, occupied by perfect people. They sparkle with all the brilliance of the brightest stars in the sky. They have bigger screens, curved screens, and higher definition than you have ever imagined. And when advertisers tell you that you deserve these things, you just might believe them. Yet your pursuit of pleasure can take you back to your own personal Egypt. You inadvertently walk into captivity to get something you think you need and know you want. Life will be better if you can just have that, right?

> Your life is more than the stuff you collect. You are here to love the way God loves you.

But all around you is the manna God provided for today. Your life is more than the stuff you collect. You are here to love the way God loves you. So, are you loving yourself or others? You can find the answer by looking closely at how much you complain.

Complaining is as natural as inhaling and exhaling. It's easy to complain about your favorite team's lackluster performance, a restaurant's poor service, bad drivers, noise, gas prices, travel delays, and weather. Complaints are rooted in the gap between your expectations and your experiences.

When something doesn't live up to your expectations, you might believe you have a just cause for complaining. Even though you don't really like to complain, you can find it impossible to stop. Why? Because you can't control what other people do, and your expectations are nonnegotiable.

So what happens when God doesn't deliver what you expect? If you are honest, you will admit that your complaining sometimes affects your relationship with God. You might wonder if He really knows or cares about what's happening in your life. Even though you don't verbalize your complaints to God, He knows they are there.

God established your identity and defines your pleasure. When your life is aligned with God's design, you'll find pleasure in the things that matter most to Him. You'll enjoy investing your resources to help others. You'll have a great time encouraging someone who has lost all hope and will be delighted modeling Jesus' attitude toward the world.

In Philippians 2:5–11, Paul wrote:

In your relationships with one another, have the same mindset as Christ Jesus: Who, being in very nature God, did not consider equality with God something to be used to his own advantage; rather, he made himself nothing by taking the very nature of a servant, being made in human likeness. And being found in appearance as a man, he humbled himself by becoming obedient to death— even death on a cross! Therefore God exalted him to the highest place and gave him the name that is above every name, that at the name of Jesus every knee should bow, in heaven and on earth and under the earth, and every tongue acknowledge that Jesus Christ is Lord, to the glory of God the Father.

Humility means saying yes to what pleases God and no to the things that distract us from honoring that commitment. When we allow ourselves to be pleased within our relationship to Christ, we find that the things that pleased us before become less appealing. We will still have a great time. As a matter of fact, you just might discover a quality of life you never knew existed.

When we live for pleasure, we often complain. Complaining isn't the attitude God wants us to have. He loved us so much that He sent His Son to die for our sins. He didn't do that so we could have a meaningless existence; He did it so we might experience the abundant life Jesus promised in John 10:10.

However, we have become religious consumers. When we attend church services, we expect quality childcare, a comfortable seat, and a speedy exit. We expect a lot and complain when our expectations aren't met. We need to exchange *our* expectations for *God's* expectations. We need to let Him take control of the life we gave Him when we were saved. If God's not in complete control, He isn't in control at all.

KEY IDEAS

- Seeking pleasure can lead to addictive behavior.
- God created us with a desire for pleasure. He gave us a world that offers all kinds of pleasures.

- When pleasure becomes our focus, coveting becomes our mode of operation. The dictionary defines *coveting* as "wishing, longing, or craving for something, especially the property of another person."

- People who live for pleasure always find themselves in captivity. It accompanies self-gratification.

- God established your identity and defines your pleasure. When your life is aligned with God's design, you'll find pleasure in the things that matter most to Him.

DISCUSSION QUESTIONS

1. What are some pleasures you often seek? How much control over your life do those pleasures have?

2. Make a list of some of the pleasures God has provided for you. Don't overlook the simple everyday pleasures.

3. How do you battle the tendency to covet what others have or do? What are some things you can do to stay focused on what God has provided you rather than on what He has provided others?

4. What are some evidences of self-gratification and self-centeredness that surface in your life? How do they affect your relationship with God?

ACTION STEPS

1. Use your journal to track the things you do that make you happy or bring you pleasure. Beside each item,

list the reasons it brings you joy and its effect on your spiritual life.

2. As you pray, ask God to help you identify some godly pleasures He has provided. When given the opportunity, talk about your contentment as opposed to your desires. Pay attention to how that shift in your conversation affects your attitude toward all God has provided for you.

chapter eight

THE SMILE OF GOD

"Life is either a great adventure or nothing."[26]

—HELEN KELLER

GOD WANTS SOMETHING *for* you, not just *from* you. That's not a feel-good statement; it's the truth from God's Word. We are here to enjoy our relationship with God. Yet, sometimes, we enjoy everything else in life a lot more. Eventually, we discover our thrill sequence wasn't all that thrilling. Life has more to offer than we realize.

THE GOD OF GRINS

We often think our way of doing things is better than God's way. Maybe you like to do things without following the instructions. Or you might be on the opposite end of the spectrum: you need specific, step-by-step instructions before you try anything. Regardless of which side you are on, there's a general consensus that instructions are necessary for many aspects of life.

Your spiritual life is no exception. You need God to tell you what to do, or you will never come close to achieving the potential He placed inside you when He created you. I love what Pastor Rick Warren says: "The smile of God is the goal of your life." You were made to make God smile. How exciting is that?

Have you ever given much thought to the things you do that make God smile? Do you even know what those things are? You might struggle with the idea that God would smile at all. You might view Him as an angry ogre, a grumpy old man, or a lightning-bolt-throwing judge. I know that one time I did a tweet about God smiling, and I was shocked at all the people who got angry even at the thought of God smiling. One person said there was nothing we ever could do to make God smile. I remember replying to him that I was sad he didn't think God would ever smile because of the actions of His children. That's not the way I see God, but maybe God smiling doesn't fit for you.

> We need to know what makes God happy. Then we need to do it.

Our images of God are formed in a variety of ways. People who were raised in church see Him one way; people who are new to the faith have a different perspective. All we have to go on is what the Bible says. We need to know what makes God happy. Then we need to do it.

It's a lot like preparing to run a marathon. Runners go through a process to prepare for the race. They know what to do to be successful and follow the plan, so they're ready. The same is true about our spiritual lives. We need to know what to do. Otherwise, we might never live up to our God-given potential. We need to understand what it means to be a disciple.

BEING AND MAKING

The word *disciple* is both a noun and a verb. Our initial calling is to *be* disciples of Jesus Christ. In that role, we are learners who crave knowing Him more and honoring Him with our lives. Once we are disciples, we get to participate in the disciple-*making* process. This is when we take time to encourage others in their relationships with God. That makes God smile.

Many Christians live far below their potential because they never embrace the noun *and* verb forms of disciple. They accept Christ as their Savior, but they stop short of becoming disciple-makers. For some reason, they believe that work is someone else's job.

Near the end of His earthly ministry, Jesus took His disciples aside and explained their responsibility as disciple-makers. He didn't want them to go through life without a clear understanding of their primary job. He offered instructions that He expected them (and us) to follow. When Jesus said, "Make disciples," He said it to every believer in every generation in every location. No one is exempt.

You might wonder how that factors in to this desire to make God smile. We make God smile when we do what He has told us to do. He gave us specific instructions that we either obey or disobey. That doesn't mean it's easy to be followers of Christ. Many people in the first century didn't get it. And it shouldn't be a surprise that we don't get it, either.

In Matthew 28, we see that a lot of people didn't understand enough about Jesus to make a decision about Him. Some didn't care if they made Him happy or not. Some didn't know what it took to make

Him happy. The crowd was confused. Even His resurrection failed to convince people that He was God's Son.

Matthew reports that Jesus told His followers to go to a mountain where they would see Him. Upon arriving there, some people worshiped Him. Others, however, doubted. How could anyone experience the resurrection and not acknowledge Jesus' deity? Many in the crowd saw Him crucified. If they didn't witness it, they had certainly heard all about it. Even then, some people didn't accept the fact that He was the Messiah. What does that have to do with making God smile?

Until you agree with God that Jesus is His Son and accept the fact that He lived on the earth, suffered a cruel death, was buried in a borrowed tomb, and was resurrected three days later, you can never make God happy. If you don't agree with Him about His Son, He will never smile at you.

How could people witness everything that happened and still not believe? How can people today have the entirety of God's Word in their hands and say they don't know how to make God smile? We know how to make Him smile; we just choose not to do it as often as we should.

You make God smile when you move from being a skeptic to being a believer.

There were people in the first century who didn't want to believe Jesus was God's Son. The facts that played out in front of them couldn't change their minds. They simply chose not to believe. From a practical standpoint, people today are the same way. They might have an interest in God, but their lives tell a story of doubt. Like many people in the first century, facts don't overpower their skepticism. Those people are living their own thrill sequence and will never make God smile.

You make God smile when you move from being a skeptic to being a believer. Which one are you? Take a look at your lifestyle. A faith that doesn't affect daily life isn't the kind of faith Jesus expects His followers to have. You can say all day that you love God, and you can even participate in religious activity. However, if your life is unchanged by God's presence, then your faith isn't real, and God isn't smiling.

Authentic faith changes everything. Some of Jesus' followers were eternally changed by the events that transpired. Their doubts were erased as they saw Jesus face-to-face. A real encounter with Christ is always life-altering.

EXCITEMENT AHEAD!

Jesus wants to send us on an amazing journey. He has plans for us that are far beyond anything we could ever imagine. Jesus knows something about amazing journeys because He defeated death. No one before Him had done that. No one since then has done it, either. His victory over death confirmed His authority over all of life. No matter who we are or what we do, we are subject to Jesus' authority. He said that He had been given all authority. He has unlimited jurisdiction. No one is outside His reach. No one can say to Jesus, "You aren't my boss." He is the boss, whether we accept it or not. He has the plans for your best life. That is the real thrill sequence you want.

This comes as news to many people who believe they control their lives and make their own decisions. Arrogance makes them believe they are bigger and more powerful than anyone or anything else. Each of us will one day fully realize Jesus is the final authority. He has the last word on everything. It stands to reason, therefore, that we should live according to His guidelines and expectations. That's the only way we can discover the fullness life has to offer.

Jesus didn't want to complicate the issue. Religion had been complicated enough. Jesus came to make it simple. His simple offer of forgiveness opened the door for people to become His followers, His disciples. Disciples are people who stay close enough to Him to learn. When we recognize Jesus' complete authority, we will look for opportunities to learn more from Him. That is the heartbeat of the authentic disciple and the path to the most amazing journey ever imagined.

Jesus didn't leave people wondering what He expected them to do. His instructions, however, weren't what most people expected. He didn't tell people to buy things or go on expensive vacations. He never told people to focus on their personal appearance or buy the fanciest car around. His assignment was universal and doable by every person.

What did Jesus assign? What could He possibly tell us to do that would bring us personal satisfaction and make God happy? Here it is: go make disciples. This wasn't an assignment for an elite few; it was for everyone.

There is often resistance to this task. Some people argue they aren't gifted in disciple-making, but that's not a valid excuse. Moses had never practiced administering plagues before he stood before pharaoh. David didn't have experience as a giant-killer before he aimed his sling at Goliath. We need to remember that our limitations are God's opportunities. God doesn't equip us in hopes that we'll find something to do. His ability follows our activity. In other words, when you step out to do something for God, He shows up. That's the authentic thrill sequence.

Too many believers are waiting for God to overpower them and do something in their lives, but God doesn't work that way. Jesus didn't say to go make disciples if you feel like it.

The reality is that all of us are teaching others about God. Some people are communicating truth; others are misrepresenting Him. The world takes its cues from those of us who claim to be followers of Christ. It's our job to help people see their need for Christ in their lives, to

> We need to remember that our limitations are God's opportunities.

mark their decisions through baptism, and to guide their spiritual development by teaching them about Jesus. It's our job to help people see the futility of their thrill sequences and the satisfaction of God's thrill sequence.

We make God happy when we are intentional about growing in our relationship with Him. When that happens, we find joy in giving of our time, talent, and resources. We will be anxious to serve and go. These activities are tangible evidence of spiritual maturation. That's what makes God smile.

Jesus didn't leave us here to figure this out on our own. He promised to be with us. Most of us have experienced Jesus' presence in our lives. We know how He enables us to do things we could never do apart from His power. When Jesus gives us an assignment, He guarantees His presence. That should make you smile. It certainly makes God smile.

Jesus never puts us in a position and walks away. You might work around some challenging people, yet Jesus is there. You might have family members who don't share your love for Christ, but Jesus is there. You might have questions about your future and what God wants you to do; Jesus is there. Through your life situations, God shows up and demonstrates His power and presence. His activity in your life should bring you great joy. And when others respond to His activity in your life, it brings God great joy.

The Great Commission is Jesus' homework assignment for every believer. We are here to make Him famous. We are here to encourage others to pursue a relationship with Him. If we do it right, trust me, it will thrill us!

Our lives will affect the way people respond to Jesus. When they see that Jesus really matters to us, they will be more likely to accept Him as their Savior. However, when people see a disconnect between our lives and our claims about faith in God, they grow more uncertain about the value of becoming a believer. Brennan Manning echoes the problem of how this disconnect in a believer's life affects the world:

> The greatest single cause of atheism in the world today is Christians who acknowledge Jesus with their lips and walk out the door and deny Him by their lifestyle. That is what an unbelieving world simply finds unbelievable.[27]

Are *you* advancing atheism or authentic faith?

We all like the idea of God blessing us. We ask for God's blessings. We celebrate great things that happen and describe them as blessings of God. Blessings are awesome things to receive. But there's more to blessings than we realize.

The Bible teaches blessing as a funnel rather than a cup. We are blessed as God's resources flow through our lives and *into* the lives of others. So when we ask God to bless us, we are asking Him to work through our lives to positively affect the lives of others. Does that change your prayers? It changes mine, and I get excited just thinking about it! I'm praying that I will be blessed to be a blessing!

God knows we are never more at peace than when we are completely aligned with His purpose for our lives. We are at our best

---

27   BrainyQuote, posted at http://www.brainyquote.com/quotes/quotes/b/brennanman531776.html.

when we are totally surrendered to Him. That's a hard truth to get our minds around. That, however, is the key to God's thrill sequence for our lives. Life becomes more thrilling when we give it back to the One who gave it to us in the first place.

What does that look like? It looks like a family walking away from lucrative careers to give their lives serving underprivileged people in the inner city. It looks like a couple bringing an unloved orphan into their home even at the objections of their extended family. It looks like a young man setting aside his career plans and forsaking a lucrative career in order to honor God's calling in his life. It looks like the young mother who chooses to invest in her children rather than return to her corporate job. All these things and more are happening, and it's different for everyone. It looks like you doing whatever it is God lays on your heart.

> We are blessed as God's resources flow through our lives and into the lives of others.

When you make God smile, your life will smile, and it should show on your face. It is a reflection of God's presence. People see God in the things you do. Your attitude changes. Your thinking is transformed. That makes God smile. Romans 12:2 says, "Do not conform to the pattern of this world, but be transformed by the renewing of your mind. Then you will be able to test and approve what God's will is—his good, pleasing and perfect will." If we want to please God, we will follow His instructions. We will resist the world's influence and honor God's design for our lives.

A 2014 *USA Today* story reported that living the "American Dream" requires $130,000 per year for a family of four. What is the American Dream? How is it related to God's perfect plan for our lives?

We can make God smile by choosing His perfect plan rather than the American Dream.

It's easy to get distracted by and caught up in the things that make the world happy. But is the world really happy, or is it just a façade? If the world is truly happy, why is there so much consumer debt and bankruptcy? Why are people buying things they don't need with money they don't have to impress people they don't know?

True happiness for us comes in a dynamic relationship with God. That relationship puts a smile on His face. Our lives become an offering to Him, and He is honored. That's the thrill sequence at a whole new level.

Are you ready for the adventure of a lifetime? Are you willing to do whatever it takes to unlock the secret of a quality of life you never imagined possible? If so, stop struggling, and let God live through you. When you become His hands and feet, you will find joy in unexpected places. You'll find it hard to follow the world's unfulfilling plan. The ways of the world will be boring; you'll be on an adventure. If that's what you want, then stay close to God. You'll never find the real thrill sequence apart from a thriving relationship with Him.

KEY IDEAS

- God wants something *for* you, not just *from* you.

- Many Christians live far below their potential because they never embrace the noun *and* verb forms of *disciple*.

- Until you agree with God that Jesus is His Son and accept the fact that He lived on the earth, suffered a cruel death, was buried in a borrowed tomb, and was

resurrected three days later, you can never make
God happy.

- You can say all day that you love God, and you can
  even participate in religious activity. However, if your
  life is unchanged by God's presence, then your faith
  isn't real, and God isn't smiling.

- True happiness for us comes in a dynamic
  relationship with God. That relationship puts a smile
  on God's face. Our lives become an offering to Him,
  and He is honored. That's the thrill sequence at a
  whole new level.

DISCUSSION QUESTIONS

1. What do you think God wants *for* you? List as many
   things as possible, and identify why God might want
   that for you.

2. What do you think of when you consider the word
   disciple? What are some ways you grow as a disciple?
   How are you actively discipling others?

3. Think about your everyday life. How do you make God
   happy? What do you do to make Him unhappy?

4. Reflect on your life over the past six to twelve
   months. How has God changed your life? How have
   those changes affected the way you interact with
   other people?

5. If your life is an offering to God, do you think He would
   accept or reject your offering? Explain your response.

ACTION STEPS

1. In your journal, make a list of some things you have done in the past that might be considered thrilling. How do those things compare to the thrill sequence God has for you?

2. Write down some of your thoughts related to making God smile. As you go through the next few days or weeks, look for opportunities to please God, and journal how you felt while making Him smile.

chapter nine

FINDING SUBSTANCE

"True contentment depends not upon what we have;
a tub was large enough for Diogenes, but a world was
too little for Alexander."[28]

—CHARLES COLSON

WE OFTEN DETERMINE how satisfied we are with life based
on the outcomes of specific situations. The day was good if there was
no traffic, no meetings, no delays, and no problems. Likewise, the day
was bad if we ran into any of those situations. It was extremely bad if
more than one of them happened.

We have been raised to live for the moment. Our lives are
one experience after another, hopefully with ever-increasing risk
and reward. Things that once thrilled us now bore us. Things that
once scared us are checked off our to-do lists. We become more and
more adventurous.

---

28   BrainyQuote, posted at http://www.brainyquote.com/quotes/quotes/c/
     charlescal104182.html.

But is the present life all there is? Will we one day run out of options for the next big thing and be relegated to a life of perpetual mediocrity and cynicism? That's one option. But there is another option. The second option isn't based on the excitement factor of your experiences, even though your experiences might be more exciting than you ever dreamed possible.

GOD'S GOOD IS BEST

Let's go back and reconsider where this all began. The story appears in the opening pages of the book of Genesis. In the beginning, God put His finishing touches on a perfect world and declared it to be good. What does "good" really mean? If God declared the world *good*, can't we make it *better*? Actually, no, we can't, because that's not what God meant by "good."

Most of the things we believe are necessary for the "good life" were not part of God's perfect world. There were no houses, fast cars, kids, money, jobs, computers, entertainment, or talk shows. There was no football to watch or shopping to do. There were no restaurants to visit or movies to see, no vacations to take or churches to attend. No parachutes to pull and definitely no fly boarding! There was a man, a woman, and a garden. Good was simple.

God created man and said humanity was "very good." He placed the man in a perfect place, and in that perfect place, Adam and Eve had everything they needed. But that's not what made it perfect. Perfection had nothing to do with what they had. It had everything to do with *who* was there: God.

Adam and Eve initially knew only an intimate, personal relationship with God. They didn't know what it was like to be self-centered. Their focus was on God alone. They were completely fulfilled in their relationship with Him. They were satisfied. So if a relationship with God was satisfying then, why isn't it satisfying now?

In the middle of the garden stood a tree—the only forbidden item on their radars. God said to the man, "you must not eat from the tree of the knowledge of good and evil" (Genesis 2:17). The reactions of two people to one simple instruction set the stage for the world in which you and I live.

For generations to come, men and women of God would look back on the events that took place in the garden of Eden and remember the fullness that is available through complete obedience to God. The prophet Micah issued a call for people to return to the garden and remember that God sets the boundaries for life. Micah reminded his hearers that God "has told you . . . what is good" (Micah 6:8, NASB). Micah's choice of words is important. He didn't say that God would eventually define *good*. The definition was past tense. Good had already been defined in its entirety.

For Adam and Eve, maintaining *good* required them to resist the temptation to eat from the forbidden tree. They had everything they needed and had one simple instruction to obey. They were fulfilled in their relationship with the Creator, so it should have been easy, right?

You know what happened. Everything changed when Adam and Eve chose to do what God specifically said not to do. Their decision to ignore God's instruction was the turning point; eating from the tree was an outcome of that decision. Because they ate from the forbidden tree, they were eventually expelled from the garden of Eden. Perfection became past tense for them—and us.

For Adam and Eve, life would never be the same. What they immediately experienced was mild compared to what they would eventually experience. Adam and Eve chose to seek pleasure on their terms, and their lives spiraled out of control. God expelled them from the garden and let them do life their way. What looked like freedom became bondage.

With the garden behind them, Adam and Eve started a family and had two sons, Cain and Abel. There is more to this story, but it ended tragically: "Cain attacked his brother Abel and killed him" (Genesis 4:8). Their decision to eat from the forbidden tree eventually resulted in one of their sons murdering the other, and this was just one of the consequences Adam and Eve experienced. Do you think they would have made a different choice about the tree if they had known how things would turn out?

Adam and Eve chose immediate self-gratification. Did they ever think about the long-term consequences of their decision? Maybe. Maybe not. We really don't know. But we can be certain Adam and Eve would have remained in the perfection of the garden if they had continued to be fulfilled through their relationship with God. Maybe Cain and Abel would have been raised in that perfect setting with a perfect relationship with God, their parents, and each other. We'll never know, because Adam and Eve chose self-gratification. They lived their own thrill sequence.

Between the time of Cain and Abel and the time of Micah, a lot of history transpired. Throughout it all, one thing remained constant: God's desire for a perfect relationship with His creation. In spite of the rebellious behavior that characterized humanity and the self-gratification that intensified daily, God still wanted an intimate relationship with His people. He still wants that today.

Long after Adam and Eve, the nation of Israel saw God's hand dramatically deliver them from Egyptian captivity, but they still chose their own thrill sequence. Their thrill sequence cost them forty years of wandering in the desert. People today are bombarded with encouragement to choose their own thrill sequences. Even though God offers everything that is really good, people still choose self-gratification.

LIVING IN GOD'S STORY

You don't have to minimize the importance of your experiences. They are, however, little more than the "cherry on top." They aren't the totality of life. At best they're dessert, and you can't live a healthy life eating just desserts. You aren't defined by the events you attend, the places you visit, the money you spend, or the possessions you have. You are defined by the obedience to God you demonstrate in every aspect of life.

You have likely heard stories about people who abandoned successful careers to pursue a ministry opportunity God laid on their hearts. They were scared. They were discouraged by people who didn't understand. The situation looked impossible. Yet, in the end, they have a story to tell that you and I struggle to comprehend.

Why is it so hard for us to let go of the mediocrity that entraps us and pursue with passion the amazing journey God has before us? Do we treasure what we have more than we desire what God has for us? Maybe that's your story. Maybe you are one of the people caught in the middle of an impossible situation. If so, here's some good news: God specializes in impossible situations! When you are at your most vulnerable, you are at the point where God can do amazing things in and through your life.

> Your life isn't *the* story; it's part of the story God is writing.

Your life isn't *the* story; it's part of the story God is writing. We are characters in His book, not the author of our own. Our lives, when surrendered to the Master, become the tools with which He creates masterpieces. He uses us for His causes. He has a plan that gives our lives value and purpose.

It's through this value and purpose that we discover a passion for living. You will never be more satisfied in life than when you are doing what God created you to do. Your life has present value and eternal significance. That's a lot of responsibility!

Your life is significant today because it is through people that God reveals Himself to others. As God works through you, you discover more about how He designed you. When that happens, your life focus becomes sharper. You have a filter through which you can sift opportunities. It becomes easy to say "yes" and easy to say "no" because you are certain about your purpose.

Your life is significant in eternity because this world is temporary. Psalm 39:4 (NLT) says, "Remind me that my days are numbered." You will spend a little time on the earth, but you will spend eternity somewhere. You get to choose your eternal destination. You can choose a real place called *hell* where you will forever be separated from the presence of God, or you can choose to spend eternity in a real place called *heaven* where God's presence will permeate everything.

Your choice determines your destination. Your choice also determines your focus while you live. When you choose self-gratification—your own thrill sequence—your life will encourage others to do the same. Whatever you have going on in your life is contagious to everyone you influence. When you choose a life committed to God, you trade your thrill sequence for the one He designed for you.

> When you choose a life committed to God, you trade your thrill sequence for the one He designed for you.

Jeremiah 29:11 says, "'For I know the plans I have for you,' declares the LORD, 'plans to prosper you and not to harm you, plans to give you hope and a future.'" God has a thrill sequence for you. His plans to prosper you aren't about dumping money in your lap; it's about giving you the opportunity to make a difference on His behalf. God doesn't promise riches; He promises His presence. When we understand the significance of that trade, we will choose His presence every time.

Unfortunately, not everyone makes the right choice. Some people choose wealth and earthly importance. They let their egos guide their thinking and lose the ability to be content. Maybe that's you. You might not be able to determine when enough is enough.

A person who lacks contentment will make unintended sacrifices. He or she will sacrifice relationships to seek rewards, parenting to gain prosperity, purpose to increase personal popularity, and pleasing God because they would rather please themselves. Those sacrifices affect the trajectory of a person's life.

YOUR STORY OR HIS STORY?

It's hard to rectify the tension between a verbal commitment to Christ and a practical commitment to self. There will always be a struggle that leads to busyness and futility. When your commitment to Christ is only verbal, your words and actions will contradict each other. You'll say you love God, but you'll make decisions that disagree with the statement. You'll claim you are fully devoted to the Lordship of Christ, but you'll invest your life and resources in things that matter only to you. You'll be confused. People around you will be confused. God, however, is never confused.

Many people hold personal points of view they inherited from their parents and grandparents. When asked to explain their viewpoints, they offer little more than, "That's the way I was raised." They have preconceived notions about everything.

Preconceived notions can derail your spiritual progress. To learn something, adults must recognize the gap between what they know and what they need to know for a specific situation. In psychological terms, this is called cognitive dissonance. Without it, learning doesn't take place.

This is where many believers struggle. They don't learn what God expects because they don't see the problem with their way of life. They don't see the difference between their thrill sequence and the one God designed for them. They don't view their problems as being that significant.

What they don't understand is the difference between the life they are experiencing and their potential. It's like scaling grades. If everyone else performs at a 75 percent level, the one performing at 80 percent gets the A.

When we measure our existence against what we see in other people, we can be tempted to settle for far less than God intended. We feel good because our lives aren't total wrecks. That allows us to take our eyes off of God's standard. We go through the motions but lack the quality of life God intended. This explains why so many people spend time in "Bible study" but don't connect it to their everyday lives. They don't think their lives need improvement; they're doing okay.

Your priorities reveal your passions. At the end of the day, you can go back and reflect on the things that got your attention. No matter what you want people to believe, your calendar and social media tell the story. You invest time in things that are important. The same is true about money—you spend money on things that matter to you.

As believers, we should desire to spend time with God. It's a natural byproduct of the Holy Spirit moving into our lives. When we experience authentic salvation, God's Holy Spirit affects our desires.

That's the path to the real thrill sequence! It's available, but you must make a personal, intentional choice to pursue it. Do you want to live a life of pleasure or a life of significance?

Many believers fail to see the spiritual implications of their personal choices because they have compartmentalized their lives. Their social lives are separate from their spiritual lives. They work hard to keep their Monday through Saturday friends away from their Sunday friends. Yet the very fact that they work so hard to keep their lives segmented suggests that they know it's not supposed to be that way.

If we go back and take a close look at the history of the Israelites from the time of their escape from Egypt to their eventual possession of the Promised Land, one fact stands out: God wanted them to learn how to walk in obedience to Him. He provided the cloud by day and the fire by night to keep them moving in the right direction. He provided specific instructions. He forgave their rebellion. Yet, time after time, the Israelites chose to do things their own way. They valued their desires more than obedience to God. They got distracted and made bad choices.

The struggle to do what God expects is universal. Paul admitted the struggle in his letter to the believers at Rome when he said, "I do not understand what I do. For what I want to do I do not do, but what I hate I do" (Romans 7:15).

Paul knew God. He was spiritually alive. His life was dedicated to sharing God's love with skeptics. Yet he struggled with doing what he knew to do. But this doesn't give us the license to live however we want. Rather, it should make us more determined to live in obedience to God's Word. That's what it means to experience God's thrill sequence.

KEY IDEAS

- Most of the things we believe are necessary for the "good life" were not a part of God's perfect world.

- You aren't defined by the events you attend, the places you visit, the money you spend, or the possessions you have. You are defined by the obedience to God you demonstrate in every aspect of life.

- Your life isn't *the* story; it's part of the story God is writing.

- You'll never be more satisfied in life than when you are doing what God created you to do.

- Spending time with God is a natural byproduct of the Holy Spirit moving into your life.

DISCUSSION QUESTIONS

1. How would you describe "the good life," and what does it take to achieve it? How does your pursuit of the good life affect your relationship with God?

2. What are some events or experiences that have helped shape you into the person you are today? What is happening in your life right now to shape you for the future?

3. If God is writing the story and your life is a chapter, what would be the introduction and conclusion of that chapter?

4. What do you think God created you to do? How are
    you bringing honor to Him through your life?

5. Based on the amount of time you spend with God, how
    influential is the Holy Spirit in your life?

ACTION STEPS

1. In your journal, list some things you think God
    created you to do and write beside each one the steps
    needed for you to start doing it.

2. Evaluate the experiences on your schedule this week
    for their importance to your spiritual journey. Are you
    doing things that help you grow closer to God or that
    distract you from doing what you need to be doing?

REDISCOVER JESUS

"One way to define spiritual life is getting so tired and fed up with yourself you go on to something better, which is following Jesus."[29]

—EUGENE H. PETERSON

ALTHOUGH THERE IS a lot of conversation about Jesus, there seems to be confusion about who He really is. Even among church-goers, there are misconceptions regarding what it really means to follow Him.

That's nothing new. Jesus approached His first disciples and instructed them to follow Him. For them, it meant walking away from their professions and families to travel with this Teacher. By contrast, following Jesus today is often viewed more like following a favorite sports team. We are fans, but we're not on the team.

---

29   BrainyQuote, posted at http://www.brainyquote.com/quotes/quotes/e/eugenehpe528422.html.

FITTING GOD IN

In the Bible, we see that when people approached Jesus, they usually wanted something. They might have thought He was a magician or had some power they lacked. They wanted the benefits of following Him without making any life changes. That sounds pretty familiar, doesn't it?

At the end of Luke 9, we see Jesus interacting with three men who all said they wanted to follow Him. In the Introduction, we talked about the first man. Now let's take a closer look at the second man. His response to Jesus suggests the man's father was still living. The man simply wanted to go home and take care of some business that was more important than his relationship with Jesus. He wanted all the benefits of a relationship with Jesus without having to change anything about his life.

Maybe you can relate. You might know people who want to fit a relationship with God into their lives. They evaluate every situation against the backdrop of personal desire. The inconsistencies in their spiritual lives are evident in their daily lives. They aren't followers of Jesus; they are fans of Jesus. The second man in Luke 9 wanted to obey Jesus—later. Unfortunately, that's not how it works. Delayed obedience is disobedience. This man wanted to wait until he had time to be committed to Jesus.

The third man in the story is similar to the first man. Whereas the second man wanted to take care of some personal obligations, the third man wanted to do something that wasn't an obligation. In this portion of the story, we discover another fact about following Jesus: a halfhearted commitment is no commitment at all.

You don't have to get your life in order before you come to Christ. As you grow in your relationship with God, you will reorder your priorities so that God's priorities are your priorities. That's the idea of spiritual growth.

But, face it, you're busy. How can you keep doing everything you're doing and pay attention to your relationship with God, too? You'll never find true contentment by trying to squeeze God into gaps in your schedule. However, when you put God into your life *first*, you'll be surprised at what happens.

THE THRILL OF REAL WORSHIP

As you grow spiritually, you'll begin to love the things God loves and dislike the things He dislikes. Your life won't become more complicated; it will be simplified. The problem is not that people are afraid of change; they are afraid of *being* changed. It's frustrating to try to hold onto the past while trying to embrace

> The problem is not that people are afraid of change; they are afraid of being changed.

your relationship with Christ, and the fear of being changed will stop you in your tracks. That's not the way it's supposed to be. God sees your potential and wants to guide you toward His best for you. Any change you experience will be a change for the better. That's the real thrill sequence.

The real thrill sequence will produce a life of worship. Worship is a human response to divine action. The Bible teaches that *worship is a way of life,* not something you attend. This might strike you as a new way of thinking about worship, but it's consistent with the way worship is described in the Bible. The Bible also teaches that God's people are to gather to worship, of course, but that gathering is simply our collective response to God's work in our lives. So what is real worship?

If you were to come face to face with God, what would you do? Whatever you would do would be considered worship. There is a difference between attending worship and participating in worship. We have the idea that the congregation is the audience, and the participants are on stage, but when we think like that, we attend church as spectators. It's more accurate to view God as the audience and us individually as participants.

When we reflect on what God has done and is doing in our lives, we respond in worship. One way we worship God is through investing the resources He entrusts to us. Maybe you've heard the word *tithe*. The tithe is a tenth part of life resources that is offered to God as an act of worship. It was practiced in the Old Testament and carried forward into New Testament times. The idea of tithing is part of the overall biblical teaching on stewardship. *Stewardship* is the responsibility to manage life's resources for the glory of God. It's our way of acknowledging God as the Provider.

You will never experience the abundant life God intends for you until you respond in obedience to the instructions and principles He has given in the Bible. Many believers today are spiritually stalled because they act as if they own everything and God gets part of what's left over. Their spiritual lives aren't thrilling because they aren't letting God guide their lives.

Here's what we know to be true: your worship is a direct reflection of your spiritual health, and your spiritual health is a reflection of your ongoing relationship with God. The quality of your relationship with God is affected by your obedience or disobedience to His Word.

Shortly before Jesus was crucified, Peter denied Him three times. In John 21:15–17, we see Jesus forgive Peter for denying Him. Three times Jesus asked Peter if he loved Him. In response to Peter's affirmation of his love, Jesus gave him some instructions. Review the passage, and note the assignment Jesus gave to Peter. Jesus told Peter (and us) to take action—to feed and take care of His sheep. That blanket instruction applies to everyone who knows Jesus Christ as Lord and Savior. In other words, there are no bleachers from which to watch God's work. Involvement is part of the thrill sequence.

God called you for a specific purpose. You have an important role to fill—a role for which you are uniquely designed and equipped. Recognizing this fact is only the beginning.

God empowers people to do the things He assigns to them, and His primary mechanism for accomplishing this is the Holy Spirit. The Holy Spirit moves into our lives the moment we ask Jesus to become our Savior. The presence of the Holy Spirit enables us to do things we would find impossible otherwise.

> You will find true fulfillment only when you align your activities with God's purposes.

You are here because God put you here for a reason, and you will find true fulfillment only when you align your activities with God's purposes. Jesus never called anyone to watch Him or to watch those who serve Him. Jesus called people to do life with Him and with those who follow Him.

Every responsibility must be fulfilled. When we are given something to do and we don't do it, the responsibility falls on someone else. This happens all the time in churches. Many people are pressed into covering responsibilities for which they aren't gifted or equipped.

You have a role to play in the church. You don't need to do things for which you aren't equipped or gifted, but you should be excited to do those things God called you to do. If you fulfill your responsibility, you will position yourself to live the best life possible.

FED UP, WITH GOD

Keep this in mind: living the Christian life isn't easy. Have you ever been in a situation where two allegiances pulled you in different directions? If so, you understand the idea of two natures. Before your salvation, you only had one nature—the sinful nature. It controlled everything you did. It was impossible for you to please God because the person controlled by the sinful nature cannot please God.

Your salvation brought with it the spiritual nature. But the sinful nature didn't go away; it's still there. So the Christian life is often hard to live because there is a war between the sinful nature and the spiritual nature. In Galatians 5:16, we see this principle: You are fueled by the nature you feed. If you feed the spiritual nature, your spiritual nature will empower you. If you feed your sinful nature, you will live according to its control.

Let's compare this idea to physical food. Most of us make feeding ourselves a high priority. Why? Because we are hungry, and we like food. So why don't we make feeding ourselves spiritually a priority? It might be because we aren't spiritually hungry, and we haven't developed a taste for spiritual food. In other words, we haven't made developing our spiritual lives a priority.

Nowhere in the Bible are we taught that spiritual growth is natural. The sinful nature doesn't like having its space invaded. Therefore, your sincere commitment to God and His ways quickly becomes a distant memory if you aren't intentional about strengthening your spiritual nature.

What would happen if you limited your physical nourishment to a snack once a week? You'd become physically weak, and your physical weakness would affect other areas of your life. You wouldn't think straight, and you wouldn't be able to fulfill your responsibilities. The same is true of our spiritual natures. A "spiritual snack" on Sunday isn't enough to sustain us for a week. Yet that is all the spiritual nourishment many believers get.

When you aren't spiritually nourished, you become spiritually weak. In a way, the battle between the sinful nature and the spiritual nature is weighted in favor of the sinful nature. You see, the sinful nature is fed regularly. You feed it without thinking about it—from the things you watch, read, and hear to your desires that are fueled by advertising, your sinful nature has no shortage of food. Even if you isolate yourself from the world, your natural mind will feed your sinful nature.

GOD: THE PRIORITY

Paul was absolutely right: it is a battle! In Galatians 5:16, Paul instructs, "So I say, let the Holy Spirit guide your lives. Then you won't be doing what your sinful nature craves" (NLT). In other words, the only way to keep from living by the sinful nature is to overpower it with the spiritual nature. Spiritual growth, therefore, isn't just an option.

Spiritual growth is your primary responsibility. If you don't make it a priority, spiritual growth will be nothing more than a hobby. That's the difference between frustrated Christians and fulfilled Christians. You get to choose which one you will be. Your choice reveals the importance you place on pursuing God.

While you may never knowingly say there is anything more important than knowing God and growing spiritually, in reality, you let things creep into your life and rob you of your time. You push some of the things you must do into your flex time, squeezing out some of the things you intended to do. Because you haven't made time with God a high enough priority, it gets put off until tomorrow—or the next day or next month. You get the idea, right?

This is one reason many people choose to start their days with God. If you make Bible study and prayer some of the first things you do each day, it will be impossible to let the day go by and not get around to them. By starting your day with God, you will give Him your attention before things get busy. The truth is this: If you don't start your day with God, there's a good possibility you won't give Him any part of your day.

In the Sermon on the Mount, Jesus addressed a condition common to all people: worry. In Matthew 6:25–34, Jesus mentioned some common sources of worry. After all, we do think about what to wear and what to eat. In fact, we probably think about them more than we should! Verse 33 is the key: "But seek first his kingdom and his righteousness, and all these things will be given to you as well." Jesus told His hearers to move God up on their priority lists to the top and to trust that God has everything under control.

> He will only show what He wants you to do when you have predetermined to be obedient to His plan, whatever it may be.

Your relationship with God requires constant attention. God really does have everything under control. He has proven that you can trust Him. Since God has a better perspective on your life than you do, it makes sense that you would consult His plan rather than trusting yourself to figure things out. You do that by investing time in knowing Him and His Word, by having conversations with Him. We call that *prayer*.

You'll hear this a lot, but it's worth repeating: God will never reveal His plan in order to give you plenty of options. He will only show what He wants you to do when you have predetermined to be obedient to His plan, whatever it may be.

Many of us have been deceived into thinking that we determine the extent of our relationship with God. After all, we like being in control of our lives. We like calling the shots and deciding what we will and won't do. That's why most of our commitments are tentative.

When Jesus called His first disciples, He called them to abandon everything they knew and to give themselves totally to something unknown. The fishermen left their nets. They didn't add a relationship with Jesus to their already busy lives; they reordered their priorities. Jesus said in essence, "fishing has its limited thrills, but follow Me, and changing people's lives for eternity will thrill you so much you won't be able to sleep!"

John 10:10 says that Jesus wants you to have an abundant life. This doesn't mean a life in which you get everything you want. It means living your life for what really matters. One of Satan's greatest weapons against us is busyness. He knows that if he keeps us busy doing things that don't really matter, we will be virtually useless to God.

You might have heard of the ancient city of Laodicea. It was located in Asia Minor (modern day Turkey). Just six miles from Laodicea was Hieropolis—home of some famous hot springs. Also nearby was Colossae—the source of cold running water. The hot springs of Hieropolis were therapeutic; the cold water of Colossae was good for drinking and cooking.

This geography provides the background for Revelation 3:14–18. The two sources of water met at Laodicea. There, the hot water was cooled and the cold water was warmed. The result was lukewarm water. It was no longer hot enough to be therapeutic, and it was no longer cold enough to be drinkable. It was stagnant and useless. So the believers in Laodicea understood the analogy that lukewarm Christians are useless. They knew what it was like to have a useless resource available, and apparently, that was the spiritual condition of the people there. They were deceived into thinking they had it all figured out. They were, in their opinion, "saved enough." But for all practical purposes, they were just taking up space.

If we believe God has our best interest in mind and that He wants us to live a life that matters, then we should listen to what He has to say. Below are some of the ways God speaks to us:

- *The Bible*—that's why it is so important for us to study it.

- *The spoken word*—such as sermons and small group Bible studies.

- *Prayer*—when we stop to listen, God usually has something to say.

- *The Holy Spirit*—what we sometimes think is our conscience is really the Holy Spirit.

- *Other believers*—God can confirm through other people something He wants us to do.

- *Songs and hymns*—many songs communicate biblical truths in creative ways.

Have you ever craved something like strawberry shortcake or a steak from your favorite steak house? Cravings are interesting because they are a result of a favorable prior experience. In other words, you can't crave something you've never had. In 1 Peter 2:2–3 we are told to "crave pure spiritual milk . . . now that you have tasted that the Lord is good." When you accepted Jesus Christ as your personal Savior, you tasted His goodness. Now what?

Peter said to keep remembering the goodness you have experienced, and allow it to increase your hunger for more of God.

Why, then, do so many believers seem disinterested in spiritual growth? They have chosen not to remember God's goodness. They were more interested in escaping hell than in living for God. In coming to Christ, they didn't want life change; they wanted an insurance policy.

We live in a world of religious consumerism where people "shop" for the elements that fit easily into their lives. They are fans of church but stop listening when God's Word steps on their toes. If they get mad enough, they'll shop a different "mall." They don't crave pure spiritual milk; they crave pleasing themselves. They really aren't living God's thrill sequence and because of that, they aren't growing, even though they've been church members (and perhaps believers) for ten, twenty, or even fifty years.

God didn't call you to be a religious consumer. This isn't all about you. You are called to be part of a holy people—people set apart for His purposes. The spiritual milk you crave helps you grow up in your salvation. Let's be clear: When you were saved, you were totally saved. Now, as you mature spiritually, your salvation will affect more of your life. As uncomfortable as it is, you must become okay with the idea that salvation will change you. If you aren't being changed, you might need to revisit your salvation experience and make sure you really invited Jesus to be Lord of your life.

As you grow up in your salvation, you will be saddened by the things that sadden God. God's Spirit living in you will make it hard to be entertained by things that violate His moral standards. You will begin to love people you might otherwise ignore. You will develop a hunger for God's truth. You will want to spend time with His people. That's what happens when God moves into your life.

It's time to move from "What will I have to give up if I choose not to follow Jesus?" to "What do I have to give up to follow Jesus?"

The sacrifice is worth it because He sacrificed His life so you can have freedom from a lackluster thrill sequence.

He wants to write an inspiring story through you. He wants to give you a reason to get up each day and serve Him. He doesn't want to take away your life; He wants to give you a life that matters!

KEY IDEAS

- Among church-goers, there often are misconceptions regarding what it really means to follow Jesus.

- As you grow spiritually, you'll begin to love the things God loves and dislike the things He dislikes.

- You will never experience the abundant life God intends for you until you respond in obedience to the instructions and principles He has given in the Bible.

- Nowhere in the Bible are we taught that spiritual growth is natural. The sinful nature doesn't like having its space invaded.

- If you aren't being changed by your relationship with Jesus, you might need to revisit your salvation experience and make sure you really invited Jesus to be Lord of your life.

DISCUSSION QUESTIONS

1. If someone asked you to explain what it means to follow Jesus, what would you say, and how do you think the person would receive it?

2. How is your relationship with God affecting the things you love and the things you dislike? What changes, if any, do you see?

3. What are the elements of the abundant life God has for you? To what extent are you experiencing that life?

4. You face a battle with your sinful nature each day. What is your strategy for defeating the sinful nature, and how effective has your strategy been?

5. Recount your salvation experience, and describe some of the ways God is making you a new creation. If you're not sure you've had a salvation experience, now is the time to fix that.

ACTION STEPS

1. In your journal, identify the tangible evidence of your spiritual journey. List some things you want to see happen in your spiritual life over the next several months.

2. Invite a friend to talk about your spiritual connections and the ups and downs of maintaining your relationship with God. If possible, make meeting with this friend a regular part of your schedule.

chapter eleven

THE ULTIMATE THRILL

"I believe life is a series of near misses. A lot of what we ascribe to luck is not luck at all. It's seizing the day and accepting responsibility for your future. It's seeing what other people don't see and pursuing that vision."[30]

—HOWARD SCHULTZ

LIFE IS FULL OF RISKS. Some people embrace them; others are paralyzed by them. You might be somewhere in between. The reality is that there are no certainties in life. Everything we do includes a degree of risk. Therefore, we should be okay with the fact that living a life of faith can be risky. That's what makes it exciting!

God created you with a specific plan for your life, and His plan is always complete. He provides everything you need to accomplish the task He assigns to you. Most people wouldn't argue with anything I've

---

30   BrainyQuote, posted at http://www.brainyquote.com/quotes/quotes/h/howardschu212497.html.

said so far. We get the idea that God loves us, but we often struggle to find that "thing" for which He created us.

ADRENALINE FOR GOD

If you've ever been involved in organized sports, you know what it's like to have your sights set on a specific role. It is often disappointing to be assigned a position that isn't on your list of desirable spots. It affects your motivation for sticking with the team, and it affects the encouragement you offer to other players.

That's how it is for many Christians. Their motivation for fulfilling their responsibility can depend on getting to do what they want. They know what they want, but they really don't understand the thrill sequence God has for them. Because they don't understand it, they stop and try to figure it out. That's not how it works. God wants to lead you on an adventure of His choosing, so if *you* get to choose, it's not *His* adventure. First Corinthians 1:8-9 (*The Message*) says, "God, who got you started in this spiritual adventure, shares with us the life of his Son and our Master Jesus. He will never give up on you. Never forget that."

What can you invest your adrenaline in? You can share your faith by changing a conversation from the natural to the supernatural to the eternal. Church will never be the same if you invite someone to attend with you.

You can give more and more. There are people who live on 10 percent and give 90 percent. People who do this are called "reverse tithers," and they are living the thrill sequence!

I know a mail carrier who has been on four continents with me doing missionary work. At home, he may be "just a postal worker," but he and his wife are living an incredible thrill sequence for God—more than almost anyone else I know!

When Christianity spread to Rome, it faced one of its hardest challenges. The Roman emperor was viewed as godlike, and most emperors reveled in that status. They were insanely jealous of any perceived rival. Therefore, faith in Jesus Christ was an issue. In addition, the Roman culture celebrated self-indulgence, but faith in God called people to reject sensual pleasures by living according to God's definition of moral rightness.

Paul wrote to believers who were part of the family of faith in Rome. He encouraged them in their relationships with each other because he understood how difficult it was to honor God in a culture that rejected Him. We can relate, can't we?

People could associate because of their common belief, but in doing so, some abandoned their individuality and uniqueness. They became part of an organization and struggled to find their places. Again, we can relate. People today join churches hoping to find a place to fit in. Paul's advice in Romans 12:3-6, therefore, is valuable for us:

> For by the grace given me I say to every one of you: Do not think of yourself more highly than you ought, but rather think of yourself with sober judgment, in accordance with the faith God has distributed to each of you. For just as each of us has one body with many members, and these members do not all have the same function, so in Christ we, though many, form one body, and each member belongs to all the others. We have different gifts, according to the grace given to each of us.

We need to view our faith as God's ultimate thrill sequence and excitedly embrace everything He has to offer.

WIRED FOR A PURPOSE

The thrill-sequence desire comes with some challenges. You might not believe you are talented or gifted. You might think others have far more to offer than you do. You might be afraid of looking foolish. It's easy to find examples of people who misjudge their talents. You've seen wannabe singers who can't sing, comedians who aren't funny, illusionists who need more practice, and ventriloquists who move their mouths too much. We laugh at their lack of talent and wonder who told them they had any talent at all.

Your real thrill sequence requires that you know how God wired you. This is how you find value in your life. It isn't arrogant or presumptuous to recognize how God equipped you. It is wrong, however, to overrate your gifts and abilities. When that happens, you step into roles you should never have accepted, and the situation usually ends badly. It's equally wrong for people to underrate their gifts and abilities. Some people do this out of humility. Some do it to garner the praise and encouragement of others.

Paul said you are gifted and equipped because of God's love and grace. You can't take credit for what God does in your life. You should simply use what He provides according to His plan, not yours. Everything God does for you is connected to His grace, not to your worthiness. You can't take credit for something God has done. You also can't set aside what God has done and live according to your own plan. When that happens, you exchange God's thrill sequence for something far less meaningful—your own thrill sequence.

The faith community is like a human jigsaw puzzle. When all the pieces are in place, it is beautiful and God-honoring. However, when pieces are out of place or missing, the picture of God it presents to the world is distorted. A world is sufficiently skeptical about organized religion, and God doesn't need more support for its doubt.

Your thrill sequence works in tandem with the thrill sequences of fellow believers to show who God really is. You have a specific role in God's grand design. Not every person is called to do the same thing. Some people are passionate about international missions. Others are more interested in local missions. Some people are great behind-the-scenes workers. Others work well with children. Some do student ministry with excellence. The point is this: when God calls you, He calls you for a purpose. You have a responsibility to God and His church. And if you don't fulfill your responsibility, someone else has to do it. This explains why many leaders and workers eventually burn out. They are leading and serving in areas in which they aren't gifted.

Spiritual gifts are the tools we use to make God famous in our world, and these gifts come with a responsibility.

In his words to the Roman Christians, Paul reminded believers of their unity but discouraged uniformity. He told them that they should be united in purpose by using their different gifts. Paul added one further element that is easily overlooked in today's church: We are accountable to one another. The body of Christ is the place where people are equipped for ministry.

Spiritual gifts are the tools we use to make God famous in our world, and these gifts come with a responsibility. Using them according to God's plan is serious business. The church in Corinth is an example of a situation in which people misused their gifts. Some didn't use their gifts at all.

When it comes to your spiritual gifts, God expects you to use them in accordance with His plan. We have a responsibility to represent Him in everything we do. There is never a second chance to make a good first impression—for God.

Sometimes it's hard for us to acknowledge our giftedness. We see ourselves as unworthy of doing anything on God's behalf. Yet the privilege of honoring God through our lives is what gives life meaning.

You can spend all of your time looking for ways to accomplish more or climb the ladder. You can buy cars, houses, vacation homes, and designer clothes and still lack purpose. You can earn trophies, win trips, run with the bulls, cram your life with experiences, rub elbows, and hobnob with the rich and powerful but return home disappointed.

The world thinks all these things give meaning to life, but God disagrees. Life has meaning when we align it with God's thrill sequence. When we help a single mom find work or provide meals for a family in need, we begin to see what it's like to live intentionally. When we study God's Word and share its truth in ways that make people think about their relationships with God, life takes on a new excitement. When we bring the good news of Jesus to those who have never heard it, life goes to a whole new level.

God loved you enough to allow His Son to die for a crime He never committed. He did it so you could have a life that matters in eternity—and today! Otherwise, He would have transported you straight to heaven. God didn't leave you here to take up space and create traffic problems. He left you here for a purpose. He equipped you to make a difference in your everyday life. Jesus lived and died for you. Now, He wants you to do the same for Him.

This is the real thrill sequence, and when you live it, you discover there is nothing like it. When you stop short of living it, you realize something is missing. Don't settle for less than the best. Don't let complacency get the best of you. You can be content with what you have, embrace the thrill sequence God has for you, and not grow complacent.

THE RICH YOUNG LOSER

Alfred Nobel said, "Contentment is the only real wealth."[31] If that's true, then our society shows more evidence of poverty than wealth. Contentment is a rare quality. Many people, including many Christians, misunderstand the role of contentment in their spiritual lives. They live beyond their means because they believe having what they want will bring them joy and the satisfaction they desire. But it never happens. A satisfied want is the seed for something else not yet possessed.

Just walk through a mall and you'll feel like you're at the fair being lured into playing a game of chance. You can get a massage, lotion from the Dead Sea, cooking utensils that pay tribute to your favorite sports team, and remote-control helicopters that will lose a battle with your ceiling fan (I know that one firsthand)—and that's all available before you ever walk into a store! The world wants to leverage discontentment against us. Jesus, however, wants us to live so much better than that. He doesn't want us to live for the world's thrill sequence.

> Some believe they can change their eternal destinations without affecting their daily existences.

Most of the people who heard Jesus speak came away changed for the better—almost everyone. There were some who heard His message, though, and resisted His challenge to their lifestyles. They wanted a Savior who fit conveniently into their lives. They wanted Jesus to bless their personal thrill sequences.

---

31   BrainyQuote, posted at http://www.brainyquote.com/quotes/quotes/a/
        alfrednobe556206.html.

Some believe they can change their eternal destinations without affecting their daily existences. That's not true, but people don't easily give up and submit to Jesus' demands. They rationalize their personal philosophies. They excuse their stubbornness. They deify their relationship with the church. Suddenly, they worship the worship rather than the God of worship. It's a slippery slope that ultimately lands them in a way of life far inferior to their God-given potential. God's thrill sequence isn't reserved for a few spiritual dynamos; it's available to everyone! I would even say it's *expected* of everyone.

There's no more appropriate story to describe this condition than Jesus' interaction with the rich young man in Luke 18:18–27. The rich young man would have no trouble becoming a member of almost any church today. Because of his status in the community and his financial resources, he would be much sought after. He lived according to biblical principles, was respectful, and had been "in church" since he was a child. But like many people today, the young man's words and beliefs contradicted each other. He spoke things he didn't really accept as true. He addressed Jesus as "God" without accepting Him as his personal Lord.

The young man revealed the quality of his intellectual training but the shallowness of his spiritual development. His choice of words suggests he understood he was in the presence of God. His actions, however, reveal his self-centered arrogance. He wanted eternal life without relinquishing control of his possessions and his personal thrill sequence. To him, Jesus was the gatekeeper to eternal life but had no present-day reality. The man was living his own version of the thrill sequence and simply wanted Jesus to be his "value-added component." Jesus isn't our "value add"; He's our everything!

The young man was certainly familiar with the portion of the Ten Commandments Jesus quoted. Jesus called these principles to the young man's attention, so he might see his life the way God saw it. The young man, however, didn't see his sin. He saw his adherence to a set of religious rules. Jesus held up a mirror, and the man still never saw himself. Of course, Jesus knew the man's heart. He understood the man struggled with greed. Every deal and every denarius thrilled the young man way more than it should have. Jesus knew the man's priorities. He knows ours, too. Like the young man, we fall into the trap of trusting more in our religious activities than we do in God's grace. We act as if God owes us something because we go to church.

The young man might have looked around the crowd and compared himself to others. He wasn't diseased, destitute, or homeless. He wasn't uneducated, socially outcast, or culturally powerless. Admitting his shortcomings in front of people whose conditions were obvious was not in his plan.

So often we fall into the same trap. We compare ourselves to others. We view our goodness in relationship to the obvious inadequacies of others. We develop a false sense of superiority and, as a result, push aside the biblical mirror that reveals to us who we really are.

When we see our lives through the lens of God's perfect standards, we often have a sudden "uh-oh" moment. No matter how good we've been, we fall short of God's standards. No matter what we've done, we've squandered far too many opportunities. No matter what we've been given, we've been selfish. We realize our thrill sequence has led us on a less than excellent journey. That's when we see our lives in comparison to God's thrill sequence. We are called to something much better than we have. When we focus our lives on God's expectations, life will be better.

"What must I do to inherit eternal life?" is a question people have asked for thousands of years. It is, however, the wrong question. You see, the young man asked what he needed to came so He could do what we can never do for ourselves: erase our sin debt. Because Jesus knew the man's heart, He knew the obstacle that stood between him and an authentic relationship with Jesus. This man had a lot of possessions. He was wealthy, and he trusted his wealth more than anything else. He had his own materialistic version of the thrill sequence.

Jesus doesn't call everyone to sell their possessions before coming to faith. He does, however, call us to give up whatever we value more than our relationship with Him. That might be a habit, a friendship, a job, or a social activity. If we aren't willing to lay down the things that own us, we aren't willing to pick up our crosses and follow Jesus.

The rich man was given the same command Jesus gave His sciples: "Come, follow me." The difference between being disciples being defeated is in the willingness to obey Jesus' simple and. The disciples put down those things they once treasured because following Jesus was more important than holding onto their stuff. The young man chose the opposite. He wanted a faith that fit into the gaps in his life. He wanted to call the shots and make the decisions. He didn't want his relationship with God to interfere with things. How absurd! Yet how common. People still want to sprinkle a little God over But that's a dish that leads to spiritual to make allowances for their busyness. uld tell them to put down what they really need.

Jesus' comments about the difficulty of rich people getting into heaven should be viewed in light of the situation. Wealth was this man's obstacle. What's yours? We shouldn't demonize wealth. We should generalize the story and see our obsessions—big or small—as giant roadblocks to our living the kind of life God wants us to live.

God didn't design us for mediocrity. We are His representatives on earth to encourage others toward relationship with Him. Our zeal for life will affect the curiosity of those we meet. Our misaligned priorities have the potential to send the wrong message to others.

When you are content with what you have, you can focus on who He is. When you are discontent with what you have, your focus will be on other things. As believers, we are called to live by a different standard. We are told to be a positive influence on the world. We do this by embracing God's thrill sequence for our lives.

The Bible is full of reminders about the power of being content. God has allocated everything we need so we can do everything He has assigned. As we live for Him, we will find the greatest joy and fulfillment. That's when life is thrilling. If God designed us, His plan is best for us.

KEY IDEAS

- God created you with a specific plan for your life, and His plan is always complete. He provides everything you need to accomplish the task He assigns to you.

- God wants to lead you on an adventure of His choosing, so if you get to choose, it's not His adventure.

- Your real thrill sequence requires that you know how God wired you. This is how you find value in life.

- When it comes to your spiritual gifts, God expects you to use them in accordance with His plan.

- Some believe they can change their eternal destinations without affecting their daily existences. That's not true.

DISCUSSION QUESTIONS

1. What are some of the gifts or abilities God has given you? What are you doing with what He has entrusted to you?

2. Is your life journey more of *your* choosing, or have you been following *God's* leadership? Explain your response.

3. How did God wire you? What are your personality traits, passions, and unique abilities? How can God use you to advance His kingdom?

4. What is God's thrill sequence for you, and how does it compare to the thrill sequence you imagined for yourself?

5. How much control do you give God over your everyday decisions? How do you know you are giving Him control?

ACTION STEPS

1. In your journal, list your spiritual gifts and unique abilities. Over the next few days, write down some ways God uses you by employing your gifts and abilities.

2. Take time to encourage someone to use their gifts or abilities in service to God.

3. Write a thank-you note to a couple of people you know who faithfully use their gifts and abilities to make a difference in your church, school, or community.

chapter twelve

AN UNSAFE FAITH

"Make sure of your commitment to Jesus Christ, and seek to follow Him every day. Don't be swayed by the false values and goals of this world, but put Christ and His will first in everything you do."[32]

—BILLY GRAHAM

JESUS DIDN'T DIE to make us safe; He died to save us. That's an important distinction.

Throughout His ministry, people often viewed Jesus only as a healer of diseases. Those who were ill or disabled heard about Him and sought an audience with Him. They probably had tried everything and were desperate for anything that might work. In the first century, most illnesses were viewed as the results of sin or curses by a person's enemy. No matter what was wrong with people, though, they soon realized Jesus was their only hope. They had

32   BrainyQuote, posted at http://www.brainyquote.com/quotes/quotes/b/
      billygraha626324.html.

tried everything the world had to offer, but their conditions were unchanged. Jesus was their last resort. Some people followed Jesus just to see Him perform miracles. They wanted to be part of the crowd without being affected by His message. To them, Jesus was a healer, but He wasn't the Son of God.

LICENSED TO THRILL

When we consider the spiritual implications of Jesus as a healer, we are reminded that we live in a time when people seek Jesus only as a last resort. People who are suffering emotionally seek advice from people before they seek Jesus. People who are suffering financially seek hope in lottery tickets and get-rich-quick schemes before they seek Jesus. People who are suffering in their relationships do many things before they seek Jesus.

Some people are what I call aggressive chasers. These are the extreme party animals, ladder climbers, addicts, and thrill sequence junkies who make normal thrill seekers look tame. Although they may not realize it, they are really the biggest god chasers, but they're heading in the wrong direction—and going after the wrong gods at full speed. They're probably meant to be missionaries or evangelists in dangerous places! What's sad is that these are the people most Christians avoid. I believe Paul was an aggressive chaser, and once God got hold of him, he helped change the world! The apostle Paul was a spiritual James Bond, except without the adultery and killing.

> The apostle Paul was a spiritual James Bond, except without the adultery and killing.

As believers, it's important that we present Jesus as our first and only source for real help in times of trouble. Although Jesus can heal, He doesn't always heal on this side of eternity. But we can always pray and ask Him for the miracle. What He promises is strength to endure the circumstances of life when the healing is delayed. If He heals us physically, we should praise Him for that healing. If He chooses not to heal us, we can still praise Him for sustaining us in this life and for giving us eternal life and healing us in heaven. That's the real hope we have to share, and it's the message of the gospel in everyday life.

FORGIVENESS FIRST

In Mark 2:1–12, we see an amazing story about a sick man and some friends who were willing to do whatever it took to get him to Jesus. They knew Jesus *could* help and were confident Jesus *would* help. The sick man wasn't carried to Jesus on a stretcher. Rather, he was carried on something that might best be described as a blanket, with one man holding each corner. If any one of them had let go of their end of the blanket, the mission would have been unsuccessful. We also get the idea that these men were vested in the paralytic's life. They probably had been caring for him a long time, so seeking healing was important to them, too. We don't know the spiritual condition of the four men, but the story suggests that they believed Jesus could heal the paralytic. And what did they do?

First, they agreed Jesus could help. None of the men could have succeeded alone. They needed each other.

Second, they rallied around the paralytic. They put his needs before theirs. They might have wanted to be part of the crowd inside the house, yet carrying the paralyzed man slowed them down to the point that when they arrived, the crowd gathered in and around the home was massive.

Third, they didn't give up. Unable to penetrate the crowd, the men carried the paralytic up the outside staircase, dug through the straw and clay roof to create a large opening, probably laid on their stomachs, and lowered the man into the room where Jesus was speaking.

How do you think the homeowner responded to the efforts of these men to get the paralyzed man in front of Jesus? I'm not sure I would have been excited if it had been my home! What about the people in the crowd who had arrived early for the best seats? Some might have been annoyed at the men for interrupting a perfectly good "church" experience and for the newly created dust storm. We don't know how other people reacted, but we do know how Jesus reacted. He responded to the faith demonstrated by these men who were willing to do whatever it took to get the paralyzed man an audience with Jesus.

Still, Jesus offered no congratulations to the men. He turned His attention to their paralyzed friend and forgave his sins. Was that the reason the men carried the paralytic to Jesus? Certainly the fact that the man was lying on a mat was evidence he needed more than his sins forgiven.

Throughout Scripture, we see how religious people were often less than supportive of other's efforts to get to know God. Some things never change. Christianity today is made up of people who prefer religion to a relationship with Jesus. They know that Jesus' involvement in a person's life causes life-change and enthusiasm. Yet people who are looking for solutions to their problems might be surprised to discover that their sins can be forgiven. The Jewish Talmud says we will be accountable for the things in this life we choose not to experience and enjoy. So I don't want to be thrilled by the world; I want my life to matter!

The Jewish teachers questioned the situation. How could Jesus forgive a man who obviously had done something to deserve his situation in life? To the teachers, the man's paralysis was evidence that he should be avoided at all costs.

When we avoid inviting people to a place where they can meet Jesus, we are just like the religious teachers described in this passage. It is easy to make up excuses for unspiritual behavior, especially if we believe we are preserving the integrity of our religion. The most religious people in the crowd were also the most skeptical of Jesus and His ministry. They were the ones who should have known Jesus was the fulfillment of Old Testament prophecy, but they were more concerned with keeping their traditions than in encouraging others to seek an audience with Jesus.

We must consider creative ways to draw people into situations where they can hear God's Word taught and explained. "We've never done it that way before!" is the battle cry of people who would have criticized the four men for their persistence in taking the paralytic to Jesus. But we must look for innovative ways to deliver God's life-changing message of love and forgiveness. Living to create a "been there, done that" list is very shortsighted. Instead, the real thrill is to create a "served there, gave that" list for eternity.

Jesus immediately knew what the religious teachers had on their minds. In Jewish thought, the heart was the center of a person's physical, mental, and spiritual life. Jesus asked the teachers which was easier to say: "your sins are forgiven" or "take up your mat and walk." Think about that for a moment. Saying the man's sins were forgiven produced no physical evidence that they had been forgiven. On the other hand, if Jesus told the man to get up and walk, there would be instant verification of the effectiveness of His words. Realizing that the religious teachers still doubted, Jesus basically said to them, "Just so you'll know that I can forgive sins, I'm going to heal this man." The paralytic did what he was told to do and walked out in full view of all the people.

No matter what amazing feat the crowd had seen, they had never seen anything like this. Has God's work in your life had this kind of effect on other people? Some people today view the Christian faith as boring. After all, many of us seem less than excited to be worshipping God. Have we forgotten what it's like to be amazed? Can we explain away almost everything that happens, so God is given none of the credit? Are we leaving the woman at the well and the paralytic on his mat?

When we pray for healing, we can't guarantee it, but we can guarantee something every time: spiritual healing. If we will participate in bringing people to Jesus, He will do a work in their lives. Then you can say with assurance, "I've never seen anything like this!"

CARRY ON!

Let's be honest: we find the time or make the time to do the things we want to do. Things that aren't critical often get put off until a later date. The problem is that we haven't made important what God says should be important; we've made important what we want to do. What's the point? The point is that we are all busy people. If we wait until we have the time to get involved with others, we'll never do it. We must adjust our priorities if we are going to make being a part of the harvest a reality. You will have to stand before God and give account for what you did with your life and adrenaline.

Where would I be today if someone hadn't taken the time to "carry" me to Jesus? Where would you be without the investment of people who were instrumental in your decision to accept Jesus as Savior and Lord? What will happen to your family members, coworkers, neighbors, and friends if you don't "carry" them to Jesus? James sums it up this way: "If anyone, then, knows the good they ought to do and doesn't do it, it is sin for them" (James 4:17). We know what we ought to do. The question is: will we do it?

Getting involved in people's lives is risky because life is messy. People are broken beyond our ability to repair them. Many people don't even know they have spiritual problems. They think their problems are rooted in something else.

> The problem is that we haven't made important what God says should be important; we've made important what we want to do.

IT'S YOUR *JOB*

The apostle Paul was no stranger to risky efforts. He took the message of the gospel to places few other believers would dare go. One of those places was Athens—a city known for its pagan religion. Paul went to Athens with one goal in mind: to win people to faith in Jesus Christ. Although the city was in decline, Athens was still an educational and cultural center. The glory days of the city were gone, and its political and commercial clout had faded. The people, however, remembered "the good old days."

Spiritually, Athens had never been the center of biblical thought. Pagan religion and mythology dominated the conversation. In Greek religion, deities were almost human. They had human desires, promoted immoral behavior, and lulled people into a lethargic state of self-indulgence. They even celebrated promiscuity.

It's no wonder Paul decided to go there and share the hope of the message of Christ. If any place needed God, it was Athens. Everywhere Paul looked, he saw evidence of idolatry and misplaced affection. And philosophically, things weren't much better. There were two basic schools of thought: Epicurean and Stoic. The Epicureans focused on pleasure. The Stoics focused on self-sufficiency. And those same philosophies, though void of the labels, permeate our society today.

Paul knew that sharing Christ in Athens would be difficult. Yet he also knew that winning Athens to Christ would ripple throughout the world. If he wanted to change the faulty thinking spreading like wildfire, he had to begin at the source.

Our culture is a lot like Athens: commercially successful, educationally accomplished, philosophically informed, and spiritually diverse. As was true in Athens, each of us connects to people who need to know about Christ and His love for them.

Awareness is the first step toward action. When we begin to think about the people we know who don't know God, we understand that something needs to be done. We can all agree on that. But whose job is it?

God doesn't show us what needs to be done so someone else can do it! When God reveals a need to us, it's because He expects us to be a part of the solution. Sharing our faith isn't a program of the church or an activity reserved for the spiritually elite. Talking about our passions comes naturally. If you're not talking about your relationship with God, you're not really serious about it.

> When God reveals a need to us, it's because He expects us to be a part of the solution.

In Acts 17:16–34, Paul saw a culture that celebrated its own greatness. The people of Athens were their own biggest fans. They were proud, egotistical, and arrogant. No one was smarter than they. They had solved every mystery known to the human race. There was no society superior to theirs. Yet Paul saw these same people destined for eternity in a real place called hell. They needed to change.

Paul went to the places where people needed to know God. He went to the synagogue to talk with the religiously misguided. He went to the marketplace to talk to the religiously disinterested. He encountered the Stoics and the Epicureans.

Knowing what Paul did is important, and knowing what he didn't do is equally important. He didn't surround himself with other believers and wait for people to come to them. But unfortunately, this has been the mode of operation for many believers. They have excused themselves from engaging with society by assembling together and waiting for lost people to wander in. The true thrill sequence doesn't sit and wait; it seeks and saves.

Our present reality is the result of past actions, and the future will look like today if we keep doing what we've been doing. Paul's faith was active, not passive. We should follow his example.

Paul didn't know *about* God; he knew God. He also knew what he believed and why he believed it. He could see the error of the Stoic and Epicurean philosophies. He knew the truth about God and was prepared to explain his faith.

How did Paul get to know God so intimately? His relationship with God was his top priority in life. Paul worked as a tentmaker. He literally made tents so he could minister without being a financial burden on the churches. He wasn't focused on his work.

In Athens, Paul identified a unifying concept: the gods on display throughout the city. From there, he put together a compelling argument without alienating those who were listening. He explained to them the identity of the "unknown god." He told the Athenians that their gods were subpar compared to the greatness of the real God. Paul was convincing without condemning. He was relevant without compromising. These are marks of a mature believer.

Paul's conversation had a purpose: he wanted to give people the opportunity to respond to God. His presentation wasn't intended to impress people. He wasn't stroking his own ego by declaring his spiritual superiority. He was pleading with people to see the evidence and draw a logical conclusion. Some people did. Others didn't.

The response of the people wasn't Paul's concern. He never manipulated anyone. He wasn't counting those who responded. Paul wasn't trying to earn a place on the list of "this year's most effective evangelists." He simply took his responsibility as a believer seriously and fulfilled a role no different from the role you have been assigned. It was Paul's job to connect his faith to life and to work that into every conversation.

People responded because Paul's life and words matched. He didn't say one thing and do something different. When our lives and words match, our message will be equally effective. Paul was effective because his relationship with God was real. When what we say we believe is confirmed through how we live every day, our reach will be extended beyond comprehension.

The early church grew without the benefit of a formal structure. It was empowered by people who were more in love with God than with anything else in life. They couldn't help but talk about Him.

Today, many churchgoers can't seem to work God into their conversations. The responsibility for evangelism has been left to the religious professionals and big events. Meanwhile, our neighbors and family members go to bed each night, stuck in their empty thrill sequences, wondering how to find hope and peace.

Inviting people to church is a good idea. However, it's no substitute for telling them about God. Suppose the bridge was out at the end of the road in front of your house. You knew that any vehicle that topped the hill would plunge into the river. Would you let people drive to their deaths, or would you do whatever was necessary to warn them of the danger?

The road the world is on leads to destruction, and we are responsible for the people passing by. It's our job to warn them before it's too late. Nothing is more important than that. It's the reason God set us here. You can do a lot of things in this life and still not have done anything worth living for.

Paul knew his message wouldn't be well-received, but he didn't let that stop him. He wasn't trying to be popular. He wasn't concerned about his reputation. He never hid his faith so he could be socially accepted. Paul simply loved God more than anything else. His life was the ultimate thrill sequence. Your life reflects the object of your affection. What do you love?

KEY IDEAS

- Jesus didn't die to make us safe; He died to save us.

- We live in a time when people seek Jesus only as a last resort.

- Christianity today is made up of people who prefer religion to a relationship with Jesus.

- We find the time or make the time to do the things we want to do. Things that aren't critical often get put off until a later date.

- Many believers have excused themselves from engaging with society by assembling together and waiting for lost people to wander in.

- The road the world is on leads to destruction, and we are responsible for the people passing by. It's our job to warn them before it's too late. Nothing is more important than that. It's the reason God set us here.

DISCUSSION QUESTIONS

1. What is risky about having faith in God? How does it change the way you interact with people?

2. Why do people seek Jesus only as a last resort? Why don't they believe faith in Jesus is powerful and relevant?

3. Based on your efforts to talk to people about your relationship with God, how important is it to you—really?

4. Why don't people wander into our gatherings looking for hope? What are the alternatives?

5. Take a few minutes, and talk about your life before you met Christ, how you realized you needed Him, your salvation experience, and what He has done in your life recently. This is your testimony.

ACTION STEPS

1. In your journal, write down your testimony, and continue to add to the list of things God is doing in your life right now. Keep your testimony fresh and relevant.

2. Make a list of some people you'd like to talk to about their relationship with God. Begin praying for the opportunity to talk with them, and keep track of the conversations in your journal.

DO WHAT LASTS FOREVER

"Only one life will soon be past. Only what's done for Christ will last."[33]

— C. T. STUDD

WHAT REALLY MATTERS in life? At the end, will you be judged by what you collected or owned? Will you be evaluated based on the exotic vacations you took, your stock portfolio, or the neighborhood in which you lived? Of course not!

God entrusts you with valuable resources that are easily overlooked. He gives you time, a personality, a brain, and influence. He offers guidance in the Holy Spirit, wisdom from His Word, and evidence of His love in creation. He cares what you do. He cares how you invest everything He gives you. Life isn't about you; it's about Him.

---

33   C. T. Studd, "Only One Life, 'Twill Soon Be Past," poem cited in wikipedia entry "Charles Studd," posted at: http://en.wikipedia.org/wiki/Charles_Studd

PLEASE: PLEASE GOD

What *should* matter to you? That's a tough question because we're all unique. Yet we spend countless hours and phenomenal amounts of money seeking guidance regarding our lives. Is it possible to honor God and thrive at the same time?

There's no other way to thrive!

In his book, *Finding Your Greater Yes: Living a Life That Echoes in Eternity*, Dr. Dan Erickson says, "I do not fear failure; I fear succeeding at what doesn't really matter."[34] We are driven to succeed. No one sets out to achieve failure! Yet our successes are not all the same. Some of our goals are measured in earthly terms—money, business, education, possessions, position, prestige—and none of these are bad things. But they can become bad if we pursue them to the exclusion of successes that would echo in eternity. It comes back to the question of influence. When we view our lives from God's perspective, we define success as pleasing Him rather than pleasing ourselves. We see people from spiritual perspectives, and we discover that our greatest joy is found in exercising the privilege of talking to other people about Jesus.

> When we view our lives from God's perspective, we define success as pleasing Him rather than pleasing ourselves.

Have you ever stopped to consider all the people and powers that influence you? Some influences are blatant, others are subtle. The truth is you are affected by outside forces, often without realizing it.

---

34   Dan Erickson, *Finding Your Greater Yes: Living a Life That Echoes in Eternity* (Nashville: Thomas Nelson, 2009), 34.

You, in turn, exert a considerable amount of influence on people and things around you. Has your mood ever affected the atmosphere at work or home? Have you ever said or done something that moved someone toward a deeper understanding of God? That's the kind of influence believers should desire to have.

Unfortunately, not all believers recognize and accept their responsibility for influencing their friends, family members, and coworkers toward a relationship with God. They might invite people to church, but they aren't sure about religious conversations. We act like the Great Commission really says, "Go into all the world and invite people to church." Jesus told us to go and make disciples. Authentic discipleship is relational.

One of the keys to living an authentic thrill sequence is taking the Great Commission seriously. Jesus didn't offer it as a suggestion; it is the basic operating guideline for your life. When you live by it, your life will have purpose. When you ignore it, your life will lack vitality. It's that simple.

ORDINARILY READY

In Acts 8:26-40, we see the story of Philip and his experience with a man from Ethiopia. This Philip was not one of Jesus' original disciples. He was one of the seven deacons chosen in Acts 6:5. The Bible suggests the deacons were ordinary men who were serious about their faith, and Philip was one of them.

It's not every day that we get instructions from angels. Yet, in this passage, an angel told Philip to go to the road that leads from Jerusalem to Gaza. For us, that would be the equivalent of being instructed to go to a major highway passing through town. The angel didn't give Philip specific instructions. Philip simply obeyed, with the expectation that God would show him what to do. It was a one-step-at-a-time approach. Verse 27 includes a phrase that is easily overlooked: "on his way." In the process of being obedient to what he knew to do, Philip encountered the eunuch. Stop and consider this for a moment. Philip's actions indicated his expectations.

Philip did exactly what the Great Commission tells us all to do: *as you are going, while you're being you, make disciples of all nations.* That had been Philip's mode of operation, and as a result, God continued to work through Philip the same way He had worked through him in the past. Living in obedience to God was Philip's thrill sequence.

Verse 27 also explains that Philip met an Ethiopian eunuch. This is significant because the man was a representative of the queen of Ethiopia. Philip, on the other hand, was a relatively common man. *Candace* was a title used for several queens in Ethiopia, not the name of a specific queen. In that day, people understood Ethiopia to be the southern edge of the civilized world. The eunuch had been to Jerusalem to worship and was on his way back home. He was not a Jew; he was a Gentile convert to Judaism.

Based on what God already had done through him, Philip expected God to use him once again for higher purposes. But because he was human, Philip would have had plenty of reasons not to talk to the Ethiopian:

- He didn't know the man;
- The eunuch was busy and was on his way somewhere else;
- They were from different socioeconomic backgrounds;
- The eunuch had already been to "church," so he must have been a believer.

Philip, however, didn't let his fears overshadow his purpose. He did the next thing the Holy Spirit told him to do: He got close to the chariot and, therefore, close to the eunuch. In these few verses, we see an ordinary man being used for extraordinary purposes. Now, that's a real thrill sequence!

Philip ran to the chariot and asked a question that opened the door for conversation. The eunuch acknowledged that he was reading but didn't really expect to understand the text. The eunuch had been to worship and was reading Scripture, but he still didn't have a meaningful relationship

> God's Word is the starting point for discussions about faith.

with God. What's the point? People who go to church and read the Bible can still be lost. As a matter of fact, those are some of the most difficult people to reach because they think they have everything figured out.

The eunuch invited Philip to sit with him and explain the Scriptures. This is an important but often overlooked part of the process. God's Word is the starting point for discussions about faith. The eunuch was reading aloud the words recorded in Isaiah 53:7–8, and he asked Philip to explain the passage. He specifically wondered about the identity of the person described in the Isaiah passage.

Philip listened before he spoke, and because he was familiar with the Scripture, he was able to connect the passage to Jesus Christ. Philip didn't just wake up one day and discover God had deposited in him a wealth of knowledge about Scripture. Philip obviously was passionate about the Word of God and had studied it for a long time.

We live in a day when we spend more time studying what others say about the Bible than studying the Bible for ourselves. We get our theology from forwarded emails and song lyrics. When placed in a situation similar to the one Philip faced, we might find it difficult to explain Scripture in a way that points a person to Jesus Christ.

Philip didn't answer the man's question and then move on to more important things. For Philip, nothing was more important than this man coming to know Jesus Christ as his personal Savior and Lord. Take a look at verse 36. The Bible says they "traveled along the road." This implies that Philip invested time in the man.

As they traveled, they talked about the implications of the eunuch's faith in Jesus Christ because he understood his need to be baptized. Philip's presentation was so compelling that the eunuch was eager to take the next step. The chariot stopped, and Philip baptized the eunuch according to what Philip understood to be the clear teachings of Jesus (remember, the New Testament portion of Scripture had not yet been written). After Philip's work was done, God moved him to Ashdod (Azotus) where he continued his ministry.

Notice the end of verse 39. The eunuch "went on his way rejoicing," because he had met God. This wasn't a coincidence. Philip ran into the eunuch because Philip was obedient to God's instructions, and once he completed his God-given assignment, Philip moved on to the next thing. He wasn't living for the moment; he was living to make a difference!

> The fact that God calls us to a task qualifies us for that task.

We need to remember that we don't have to be "qualified" to be used by God. The fact that God calls us to a task qualifies us for that task. In other words, God doesn't call us to do things He doesn't empower us to do. We also must keep in mind that God's instructions will never contradict what He has revealed in Scripture. Therefore, we can trust Scripture to validate the things we believe God calls us to do.

Philip didn't have an elaborate strategy for sharing his faith. He simply met people where they were, listened, explained to them their need for Jesus, and stayed with them until God moved him. For Philip, it was never about the quantity of believers his ministry produced. He apparently understood that the quality of a person's encounter with Christ was much more important.

People are aware that churches exist; they just aren't sure there are authentic believers inside the churches. They aren't looking for a place to attend; they are looking for solutions to real-life problems.

As a Christ-follower, you have an obligation to invest in other people. When God reveals a need to you, it's your assignment. God doesn't show you the needs He wants someone else to meet. When you focus on loving others, your life will be thrilling, and you'll discover more about your purpose.

A popular praise song says, "They will know we are Christians by our love." It was written in 1968 by a Catholic priest named Peter R. Scholtes and based on Jesus' words in John 13:35: "By this everyone will know that you are my disciples, if you love one another." If we want people to know we are Christ's disciples, love is the way to show it.

NOW AND FOREVER

How much time do you have left on earth? You can't know the answer to that question. So how much time you have left isn't the issue; what you do with the time is what really matters. Eventually, you will account for the time God gave you. The unfortunate truth is that you can't go back and relive any moment of your past. The encouraging truth is that you can choose how to live the remainder of your days. Starting today, you can redesign your future and live with renewed focus and intentionality. You can enter God's thrill sequence.

If yesterday's decisions contributed to today's experiences, then today's decisions will affect tomorrow's experiences. That's a simple, universal principle that often goes unheeded. People still make choices that set them up for unpleasant circumstances. They know what they should do yet they choose not to do it. There are many ways to describe those people, but the Bible calls them fools.

If you don't want to be categorized as a fool, you must start making better choices. Paul said to resist being "conformed to the pattern of this age" (Romans 12:2). Decide now to adopt God's thrill sequence for your life. He put you here for a reason. Your salvation is partly about your eternity and partly about your present reality. We tend to focus more on eternity than our day-to-day responsibilities. In 1 Peter 4:1–11, Peter advises us to take our responsibilities seriously.

So what are our responsibilities? We should understand that our resistance to the world's ways will not endear us to nonbelievers. They don't understand us because they don't have the same frame of reference as we do. Some will shake their heads in disbelief at our choices; others will be more abusive than that.

If you know what to expect, you can prepare to respond. There's a tension, however, between your desire to honor God and your desire to interact with your friends. Weak believers give in to the most visible pressure. Because God can't be seen and their friends can, they will choose to go along with their friends. What's the big deal?

When you agree with your unbelieving friends, you send a message to them about the value of your relationship with God. If there is a disconnect between what you say you believe and what you do, they will make up their minds based on your actions.

Peter explained the problem by pointing out that all people will stand before God for judgment. When you compromise the faith by imitating the world, you encourage people to dismiss God's call to repent. They are less likely to accept God's offer of forgiveness if they see people who claim to be believers living as if their faith doesn't matter. You have a responsibility to live as if your faith does matter.

It should affect the way you handle every situation in life. Pointing people to Jesus isn't the responsibility of a few people who work at the church. It's the responsibility of everyone who claims to know Jesus Christ as Lord and Savior.

Apparently, Peter dealt with the cultural tendency to live a secret faith. He saw believers trying hard to fit into the world, and he warned them to be careful. First Peter 4:10 is worth a closer look in this regard. Peter said, "Each of you should use whatever gift you have received to serve others, as faithful stewards of God's grace in its various forms."

What gift have you received? You probably know without having to take a survey. You know the things you do that give you a sense of contribution and purpose. You know when you are using your life in a way that brings honor to God.

So why do many believers waste their lives sitting on the sidelines? Why have so many "retired" from serving God? They probably missed what Peter said in verse 11: "If anyone serves, they should do so with the strength God provides, so that in all things God may be praised through Jesus Christ." Peter said we should let God be praised through all things. That means all of life. Your thrill sequence is to honor God forever!

In Luke 9:25, Jesus said, "What good would it do to get everything you want and lose you, the real you?" (*The Message*). The real you is the eternal part. It's the part of you that will last into eternity. You have a choice. You can choose eternity with God in heaven, or you can choose eternity separated from God. You can have it all and then lose the only thing that matters—your soul.

You are on this earth because God decided you should be here. His grand plan gives you a place and a purpose. When you step into the role He has for you, you will experience your best possible life. That means you must be committed to serving Him with your entire life. You must be willing to push back against the social pressure to conform to the world's standards. You must make honoring God more important than anything else you do.

What's the other option? You can live far below your potential by pursuing your own thrill sequence. You can waste your adrenaline, squandering the resources God entrusted to you by investing them in things that matter to you but not to Him. You can live to honor yourself or live to honor Him. There's only one wise choice: God's thrill sequence. It's time to go *all in* and find thrills that truly satisfy!

KEY IDEAS

- God entrusts you with valuable resources that are easily overlooked.

- When we view our lives from God's perspective, we define success as pleasing Him rather than pleasing ourselves.

- One of the keys to living an authentic thrill sequence is taking the Great Commission seriously.

- We need to remember that we don't have to be "qualified" to be used by God. The fact that God calls us to a task qualifies us for that task.

- Starting today, you can redesign your future and live with renewed focus and intentionality.

- You can live to honor yourself or live to honor God. There's only one wise choice. It's God's thrill sequence!

DISCUSSION QUESTIONS

1. What are some of the resources God has entrusted to you, and how are you using them? Are you honoring God with them or using them for your own benefit? Explain your response.

2. How do you define success? Is it all about what you get or how you live? Talk about your response.

3. What is your reaction to the Great Commission? Why do many believers choose to disobey it?

4. What is something God has asked you to do for which you don't feel qualified? What happened when you responded in obedience to His calling?

5. If you could design your future, what would it look like, and how would you invest your life? What is keeping you from doing what you described?

6. What is God's thrill sequence for your life? How does it compare to your own thrill sequence?

ACTION STEPS

1. In your journal, keep notes regarding the "God moments" you have as you pursue His thrill sequence for your life.

2. List the people God has given you to influence, and list some of the ways you are encouraging them in the pursuit of their God-given thrill sequence.

ABOUT THE AUTHOR

ROB KETTERLING is the founder and lead pastor of River Valley Church, a multisite church started in Minnesota in 1995. It has since grown into a thriving church with over 5,000 in attendance across five U.S. campuses and one international campus in Valencia, Spain, with further expansion plans in its future. Rob serves on several church and para-church boards, including the Board of Regents at North Central University, and is on the lead team of the Association of Related Churches (ARC). He is the author of *Change Before You Have To.*

Rob and his wife, Becca, live in Minnesota with their two boys, Connor and Logan. You can follow Rob on Twitter (@robketterling), Facebook (robketterling), and through his blog (robketterling.com).